Sign in | Basket

My Account My Purchases Advanced Search Browse Collections Rare Books Art & Collectibles Textbooks Sellers Start Selling Help CLOSE   9789793780139   ✕

Search Results   **Warwick Purser**

Stock Image

View Larger Image

Made in Indonesia: A Tribute to the Country's Craftspeople
Warwick Purser

ISBN 10: 9793780134 / ISBN 13: 9789793780139
Published by Equinox Publishing, 2005
Language: English

[NEW] [CONDITION: NEW] [HARDCOVER]

Save for Later

From **The Book Spot**, Sioux Falls, SD, U.S.A.
(5-star seller) ★ ★ ★ ★ ★
AbeBooks Seller since February 5, 2013
View this seller's items

View all 4 copies of this book

| 1 New from US$ 59.00 | 3 Used from US$ 36.54 |

Filter by: Dust Jacket (1) Hardcover (4) First Edition (1)

Buy New

US$ 59.00
Convert Currency

Shipping: Free Shipping
Within U.S.A.
Destination, rates & speeds

Quantity: 1 available

Add to basket

30 Day Return Policy

About this Item

Seller Inventory # Abebooks494131

Contact seller

Report this item

Bibliographic Details
Title: Made in Indonesia: A Tribute to the ...
Publisher: Equinox Publishing
Publication Date: 2005
Binding: Hardcover
Condition: New

About this title
Synopsis:
Any stroll through the streets frequented by people in Indonesia's tourist centers or markets throughout the country will uncover thousands of hand-made products, many of them of questionable design and quality. Most people's judgment of Indonesia's handcrafted products is based on this experience. What is much less known, however, is that Indonesia contains some of the world's most talented craftspeople who are busy producing high quality products that sit on... + More

Store Description

Visit Seller's Storefront

Seller's business information
The Book Spot
MN, U.S.A.

Terms of Sale:
We guarantee the condition of every book as it's described on the Abebooks web sites. If you're dissatisfied with your purchase (Incorrect Book/Not as Described/Damaged) or if the order hasn't arrived, you're eligible for a refund within 30 days of the estimated delivery

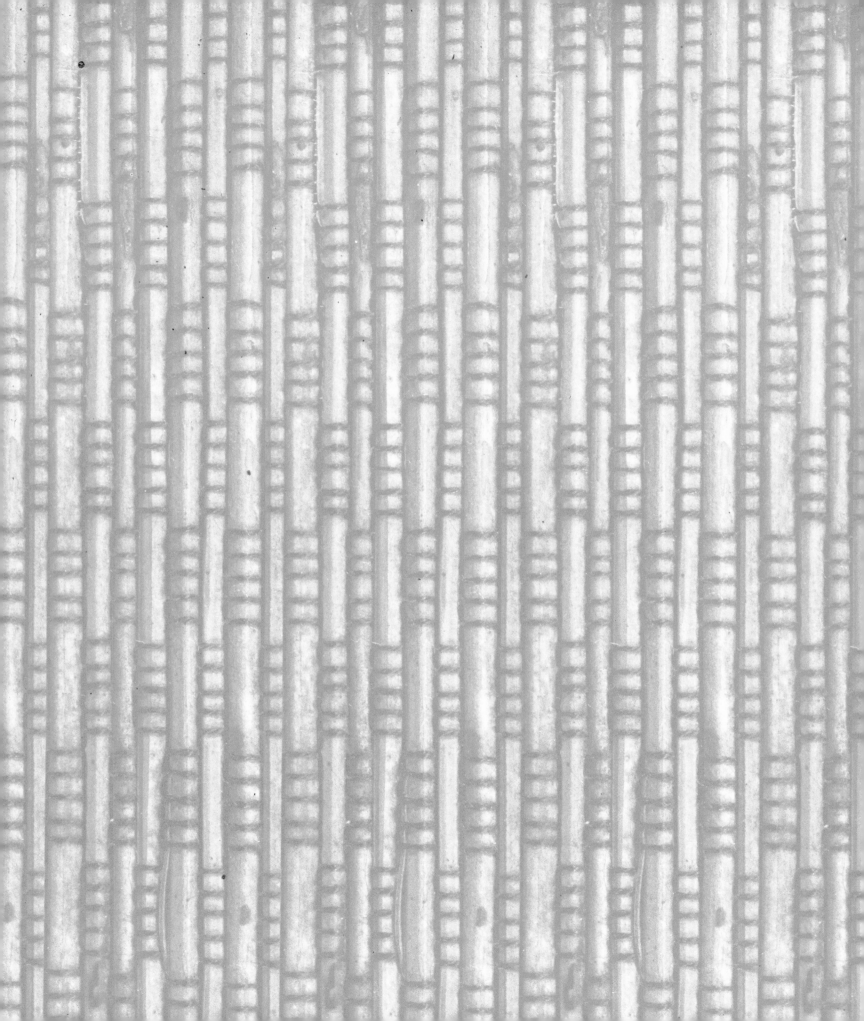

MADE IN INDONESIA

WARWICK PURSER

MADE IN INDONESIA

A Tribute to the Country's Craftspeople

photography by Rio Helmi

EQUINOX
PUBLISHING
JAKARTA   SINGAPORE

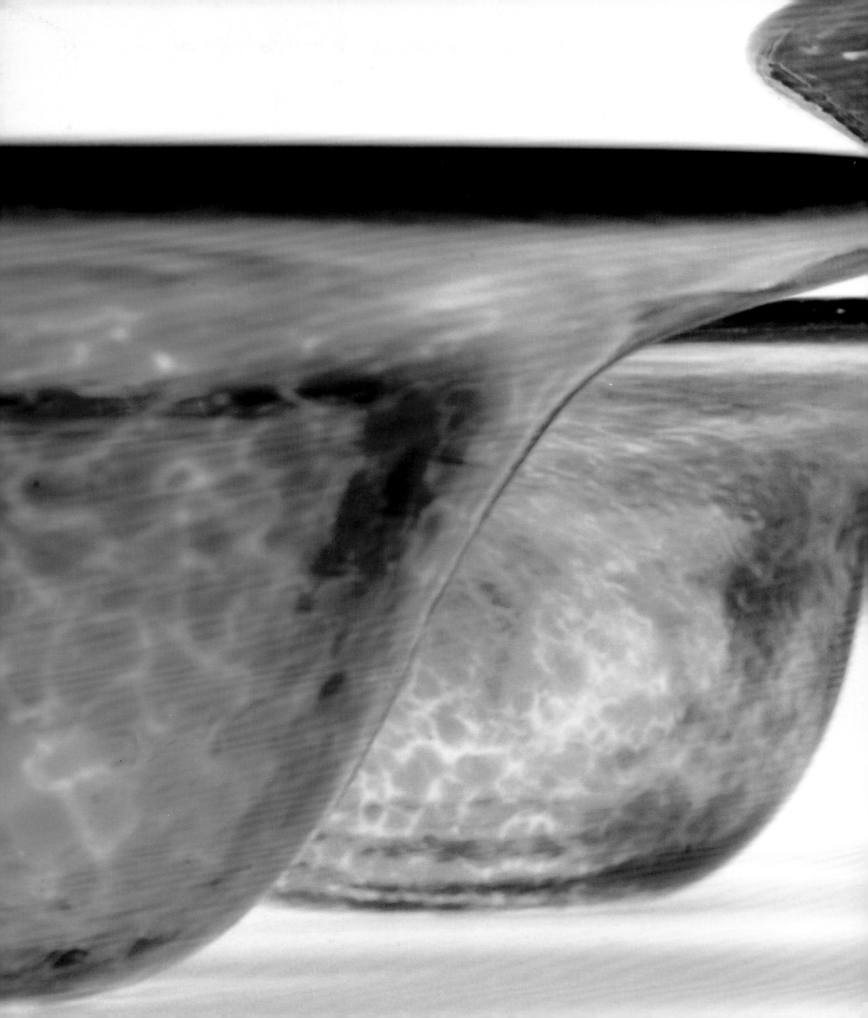

PT Equinox Publishing Indonesia
Menara Gracia 6/F
Jl. HR Rasuna Said Kav. C-17
Jakarta 12940

www.EquinoxPublishing.com

MADE IN INDONESIA: A Tribute to the Country's Craftspeople
by Warwick Purser

ISBN 979-3780-13-4

text ©2005 Warwick Purser
photos ©2005 Rio Helmi
text editor: Michelle Chin
photo stylist: Polly Purser

Printed by Jayakarta Agung Offset

Produced with the kind support of HSBC Indonesia

TABLE OF CONTENTS

◀ *Woven paper chair and ottoman. courtesy of Disini*
◀◀ *Glass bowls. courtesy of Jenggala*
opposite title page *Bedset and bag. courtesy of Disini*
half title page *Resin lamps. courtesy of Produs Trend*

INTRODUCTION

▲ *Detail of woven* lontar.

◄ *Balinese women weaving* lontar.

Indonesia is blessed with a vast resource of natural assets. Its extraordinarily beautiful scenery of volcanic hills and lush green fields harbors a wealth of mineral deposits and natural materials. It is populated by a warm, friendly and generally industrious people. These people, who live by the traditions of many diverse indigenous cultures, possess that most special and often overlooked resource – the ability to make beautiful objects with their hands.

For centuries, the utilities required for practical daily life have been fashioned from the abundance of available natural materials. Today, the skills and creativity of these craftspeople have attained a level of such quality that their creations are to be found in some of the best known retail stores in the world.

◀ Mendong *drying in the sun before being processed for weaving.*

An Abundance of Materials

Indonesia has an abundance of natural materials, many of which are unique to this country. These include fibers such as pandanus, *agel* (a type of palm leaf), *mendong* (a reed-like grass), water hyacinth that grows in rivers and lakes throughout Indonesia, and scented vetiver or cedar roots. There are plant materials such as bamboo, rattan and coconut, and stone materials such as volcanic lava rock and tuff, colorful limestone marbles, and various types of clay used to make terracotta.

Add to this a range of supplementary materials such as leather, glass, metal and resins and the instinctive creativity of Indonesia's craftspeople and the possibilities for attractive accessories and artworks are seemingly endless.

Indonesians are capable of converting waste materials such as soft drink cans, newspapers and magazines, scrap metal and plastic into items that are both practical and attractive and desirable in an increasingly "environment aware" marketplace.

Imagine a half meter high, shimmering peacock intricately fashioned from used soft drink cans; recycled magazines transformed into colorful, chic carry bags that will later be sold in shops in the south of France; smart, contemporary desk accessories incorporating recycled newspaper; attractive and sturdy plant holders or fruit bowls woven from recycled aluminum; bathroom accessories created with the leftover metal from the manufacture of bicycle chains; and storage containers crafted from used plastic strapping.

Indonesia's natural materials need to be protected to ensure sustainability and maintain its advantage over neighboring producers, and the skills of its craftspeople need to be encouraged and more widely appreciated.

Skilled Craftspeople

Any day, anywhere in Indonesia, there is ample evidence of the intrinsic skills of its craftspeople. We see it in the intricacy of woven bamboo baskets used in everyday life throughout Java, in hand molded terracotta utensils in households in Lombok, and in the finely embroidered silk *songket* worn in South Sumatra. We can admire the beauty of offerings prepared by the Balinese for their temple ceremonies.

Hence the craftsmanship continues to be passed from one generation to the next and, along the way, these ancient skills are adapted by those who are aware of the opportunities beyond their local borders. And so, modern accessories and furnishings based on traditional craftwork find their way into homes in Europe, America, Australia and across Asia.

◀ *Black and white pebble chair. Courtesy of Carlo.*

▶ *Stone carving in Bali.*

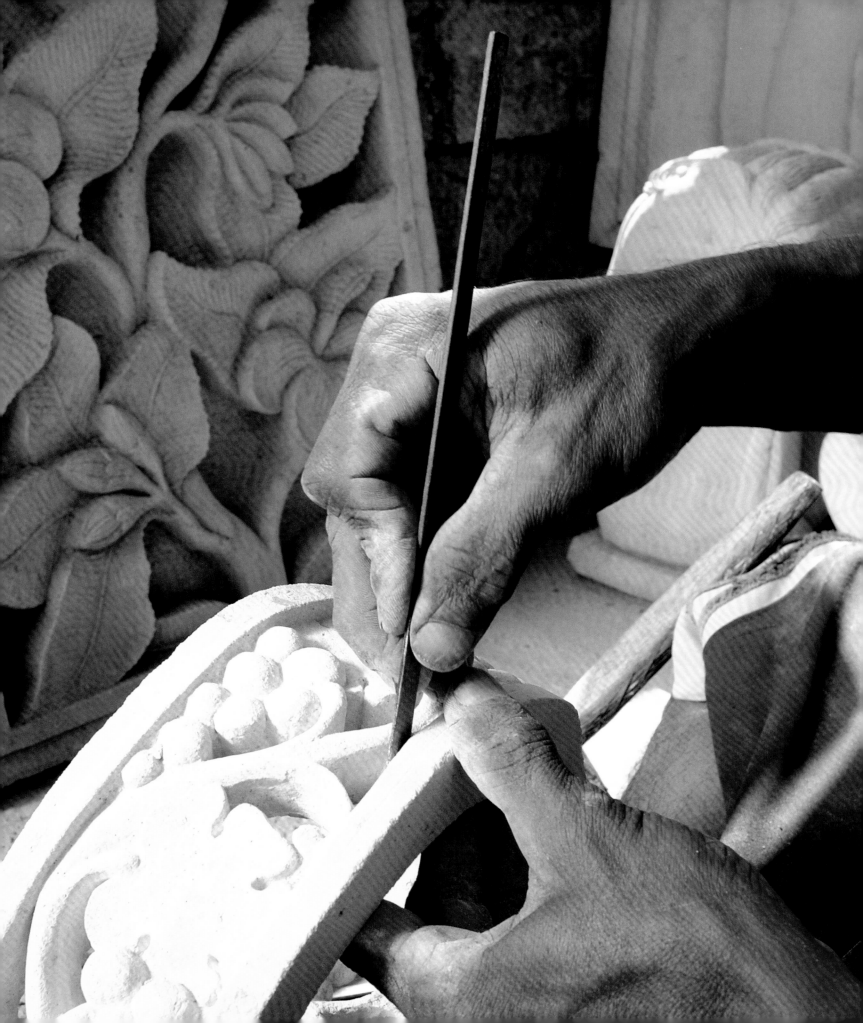

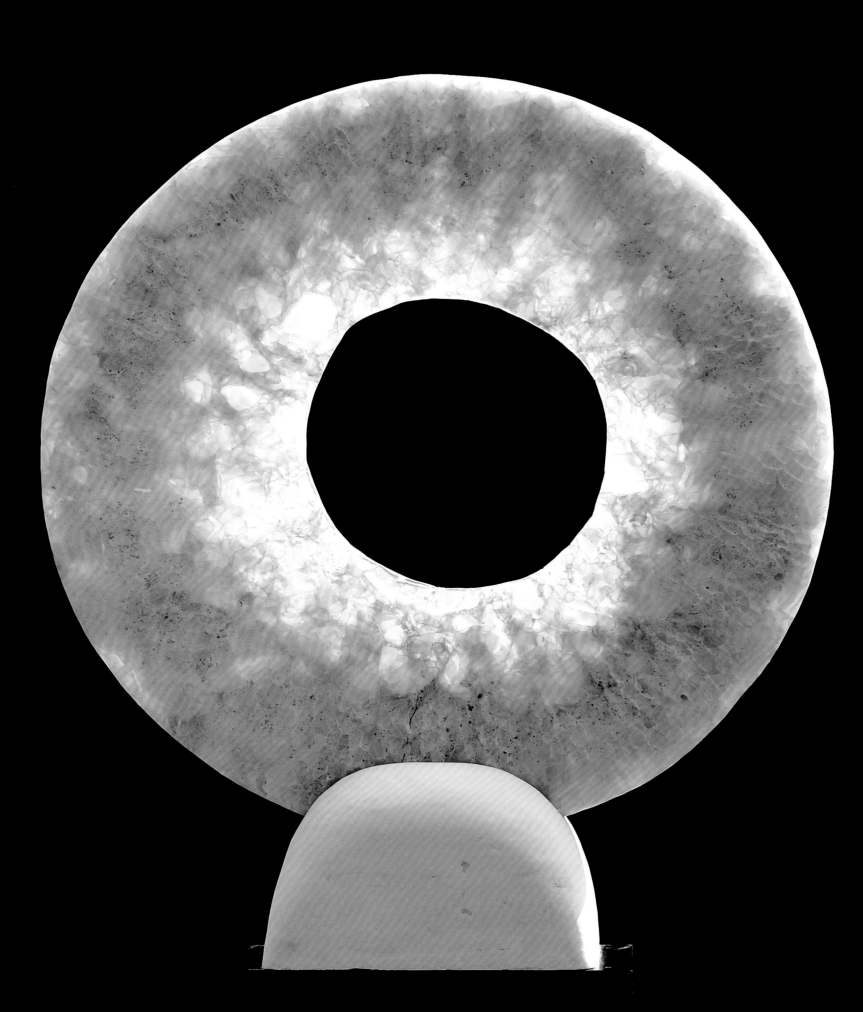

Throughout this book I try to avoid using the word "handicrafts". Although the tourist souvenir market is important to Indonesian craftspeople, I feel it is wrong to relegate to handicraft or souvenir status many of the items that are produced for export. For instance, I don't consider it appropriate to classify a Harrods Christmas hamper made in Yogyakarta as a handicraft item. And equally with household items made in central Lombok and sold in Habitat, or natural fiber packaging created for Crabtree & Evelyn and The Body Shop, or marble household accessories made in East Java for Marks and Spencer and Pottery Barn, or pandanus placemats made in West Java for Crate & Barrel.

Whether they be handicrafts bought by tourists as souvenirs from road-side stalls or handmade items gracing the shelves of the beforementioned world's great retailers, each is the result of the workmanship of a craftsperson working from a home or workshop located in a simple village in a rural area of Indonesia.

▶ Mendong *packaging used by Crabtree & Evelyn*

◀ *Cast glass ring on stone base by Seiki Torige. courtesy of Galeri Esok Lusa*

Innovative and Creative Designs

In general terms, Bali is the showcase for Indonesia's handmade products and the major source of inspiration for artistic creativity. A stroll along the main streets of Seminyak and Legian provides ample evidence of this, with many shops displaying world-class interior products. Although some of these products may never find their way out of the country, many also are exported overseas, and many of these shops would not look out of place in the smartest shopping centers of the world.

The main reason that Bali is the major source innovative design is due to the Balinese themselves. Their creativity is evidenced everywhere in the basic elements of their lifestyle, from the daily religious offerings made in every household to an elaborate temple festivals. Their wood and stone carvings, the brilliance and diversity of the clothing that they wear for festive occasions, and the manner in which they decorate their houses all bear witness to the fact that very few places in the world equal Bali for the depth of its artistry.

During the 1930s and 1940s, foreign artists such as Walter Spies, Rudolf Bonnet and Adrien-Jean Le Mayeur de Merprès came and settled in Bali and greatly influenced the work of local artists. More recently in the 1960s the Dutch artist Arie Smit was a major influence. The "Young Artists" style of painting originated in Bali as a result of exposure to his works. Similarly, expatriate designers who came to Bali in the 1970s and 1980s have also played an important role in influencing the design of Indonesian handcrafted products.

▶ *Ceramic plates and bowls. courtesy of Jenggala.*

◄ *Knockdown bamboo and glass table. courtesy of Linda Garland*

As an example, the Irish-born interior designer Linda Garland is one of the most important pioneers in the development of modern designs for bamboo furniture and household items. She was perhaps the first expatriate residing in Bali to make a strong impact on the design of local handicrafts.

Made Wijaya (born Michael White in Sydney, Australia) arrived in Bali in 1973. He is internationally recognized for his extraordinary skill in landscape gardening, and his gardens are often filled with his highly innovative and attractive accessories made from stone and other materials.

Canadian-born John Hardy creates beautiful jewelry in a fascinating workshop employing hundreds of craftspeople in a Balinese village outside of Ubud. In 1975, during the course of a round-the-world trip, he stopped at the island of Bali and settled there. Today John Hardy's jewelry and homeware are found in the most sophisticated department stores of the world, such as Neiman Marcus and Saks Fifth Avenue.

Carlo Pessina has been making interior furniture and other products made from coconut shell inlay since 1982. His creations transform the ubiquitous fruit of a palm tree into art pieces of extraordinary beauty.

These particular people have lived in Bali for twenty years or more and their presence continues to have a strong influence on what is produced by hand on that island. In recent years they have been joined by many other creative foreign designers who provide employment to a total combined work force in Bali numbering in the many thousands.

◀ *Detail of* lontar *weaving.*

▶▶ *Black terracotta plates, vases and bowls with palm leaf. courtesy of Out of Asia.*

Employment Opportunities

Throughout Indonesia, the business of handcrafted products provides employment for hundreds of thousands of people. It is not known exactly how many craftspeople in Java are kept in full employment but my own company can account for 10,000 workers, so I presume that the total number is many times that number.

Java is the main production center for many Indonesian handcrafted products that are exported, and Yogyakarta, Java's cultural capital, can justifiably be called the "center" of Indonesia's handicraft industry. In Yogyakarta, tens of thousands of craftspeople are employed working in various materials in centers spread throughout the city and neighboring districts. The activities of handicraft production spread well beyond Yogyakarta too: west to Tasikmalaya for products made from pandanus and east to Tulung Agung for marble items.

Invariably, employment opportunities generated by the business of handcrafted products occur where they are most needed in the rural areas. In the villages of these areas of Indonesia, too often people are either unemployed, or under-employed due to the seasonality of agricultural life. Many leave their homes in the villages to seek employment in the cities where they augment the already overpopulated urban centers. This move into the cities also changes the basic structure of Indonesian family life so integral to the culture of this country.

It is both the sheer number of people involved in this industry and the way in which the income earned can so dramatically improve their living standards never ceases to impress me. I live with the evidence of these employment opportunities on a daily basis. My home base is in the village of Tembi on the outskirts of Yogyakarta. Tembi is a typical Javanese *kampung* inhabited by simple, charming people who derived small incomes from agricultural pursuits. But sadly, as rural lands were encroached by urban development, and incomes diminished while the cost of living increased, many people were forced to seek employment in the big cities. Their chance to enjoy a basically healthy lifestyle in the village was sacrificed for the deprived living standards in the poor areas of cities where in most cases they were still unable to find employment.

When I first moved to Tembi, the streets were unpaved as is still the case in many villages in Java. Many of the houses in Tembi – wonderful examples of traditional Javanese architecture – were sadly in dire need of repair. Many families could not afford to buy day-to-day basics or provide education for children. It would seem that there were very few assets that could ensure any degree of continuous and sustainable living. There was, however, the one asset to which I have referred: the ability Indonesians have to create almost anything and everything with their hands. Tembi was no exception. However, while the skills were there, they were not being properly utilized. My challenge was to revitalize this talent in an effort to improve their standard of living.

▶ *Applying molten glass ornamentation to a handblown chalice.*

◄ *Covering containers with woven pandanus.*

It took some time, but present-day Tembi is a hive of activity. There are workshops producing pandanus placemats for Macys, vases for Crate & Barrel, storage items for Harrods, and many other handcrafted products. Most importantly, the advantages derived from these activities are evidenced everywhere. People have returned from the cities to their home village because there are now opportunities for employment. Roads are paved, houses have been restored, and all the children now receive an education. There is also a foundation funded by my company that provides most of the daily living needs for the forty or so families which are unable to support themselves.

It is this daily evidence of a complete change of life style – not just in Tembi, but in many other villages where the business of handcrafted products has provided employment – that gives me not just an outlet for any creative talent I might have but more importantly, a passion for my work. People often say, "How grateful these people must be for what you have done to their lives." I can assure you that it is I who feels grateful. How fortunate I am in my later working years, that through these people and their talent, I have been able to find an amazing source of passion for work specifically and life in general.

◀   *Dying* agel *fiber*

▶   *Dyed and woven* agel *fiber*

◀ *Detail batik on silk motif.*
courtesy of Ardiyanto

Economic Advantages

The enormous economic advantages of the industry in which I work are still largely unrecognized at many levels. In a country where there is considerable unemployment, expanding the industry to provide more work opportunities is relatively easy when compared to other businesses. When most businesses need to expand they have to invest large sums of money in equipment and other facilities to cope with an increase in production. In the business of handcrafted products, skilled hands replace equipment so the investment is minimal. Certainly some investment and time is required for training so that what the craftspeople produce meets the market's requirements in terms of design, quality, production and delivery deadlines.

I started Out of Asia over ten years ago. It had very humble origins but now it has grown to be one of the largest exporters of handmade products in Southeast Asia. There were endless problems in the early days. Working with skilled craftspeople and having amazing materials with which to work is a great start. The big challenge however was in getting the craftspeople to commit to production deadlines and to understand the international market's quality and design standards. In the early days our failures matched our successes. I am proud to say that now all of our own craftspeople and most of those working with our subcontractors have learned to meet our requirements. Our quality-rejection rate in the early days could be as high as fifty per cent. It is now down to about three. Many thanks are due to my dedicated staff and the intensive training programs that they organized.

Buying "Made in Indonesia"

When marketing our products we continually look for new markets, but one of the biggest markets happens to be right on our doorstep. Perhaps one day in Indonesia consumers will realize that "buying Indonesian" as opposed to "buying foreign" can help provide work opportunities in a country where there is still considerable unemployment.

"Made in Indonesia" is something we all need to embrace with greater pride. Lining the shelves of internationally famous stores, and labeled "Made in Indonesia", these products are wonderful exponents of Indonesia's culture and skills. If a customer in a store picks up a beautiful, intricately-made household item labeled "Made in Indonesia", a desire is immediately instilled to know more about or even visit the country of its origin.

This book is dedicated to the craftspeople, and the amazing products contained herein reflect their skill, ingenuity and resourcefulness while paying tribute to the fascinating culture of the country I am pleased and proud to call my home – Indonesia.

▶ *Detail of silver jug with chalice. courtesy of John Hardy*

▶▶ *Detail of steel lamp. courtesy of Upnormal*

TERRACOTTA AND CERAMICS

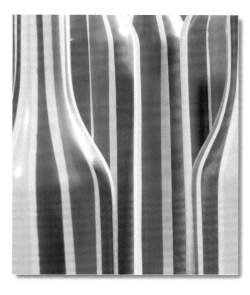

▲ *Detail of painted terracotta bottles.*

◀ *Ceramic wheel work.*

There is a long history of Indonesians using terracotta and ceramics for both household use and statuary dating back to the Majapahit period more than 800 years ago. Archaeological excavations continue to unearth basic household items made from these materials that are many centuries old.

The soil that is the basis for terracotta is usually taken from heights well above sea level, often from the slopes of mountains. Once dried, the soil is beaten until it becomes smooth and then soaked in water. This wet clay-like material is mixed with fine, dry earth and molded into various shapes for many uses.

The availability of the basic clay substance is widespread throughout Indonesia, particularly in parts of Java and Lombok and to a lesser extent, Bali. In Bali it is most often used as ornamentation on the roofs of temples and houses, as well as decorative wall panels or simple oil lamps.

In Java and Lombok, however, thousands of people are employed in the making of terracotta items ranging from small candleholders to large garden pots. In Lombok there are approximately 3,000 craftspeople producing terracotta items and probably as many part-time workers.

In Java, the two main production areas are Pleret and Kasongan just outside Yogyakarta. In Pleret the range of design is perhaps more limited when compared to other production areas but the quality is very high. The main street of Kasongan, which runs for several kilometers, is full of shops selling items of innovative styles and finishes of varying qualities and prices. Compared to Lombok, the finished design of Kasongan terracotta tends to depend more on the addition of other natural materials to the finished shape: vases covered with rattan, pots wrapped with water hyacinth, and other items that have been innovatively painted.

In Java, terracotta is baked in ovens to a temperature of 1,000 degrees whereas Lombok terracotta still employs the traditional method of baking in ground ovens where temperatures reach no more then 400 degrees. Despite the traditional method of production, it is probably in Lombok that terracotta production reaches its highest level of creativity in Indonesia.

Black terracotta vases. courtesy of Out of Asia

Detail of black terracotta vases.

One example of Lombok's creative finishes is application of the juice of the tamarind fruit. The juice is sprayed on the dried terracotta, producing a dappled look that varies from the appearance of a wood finish to the skin of an exotic jungle animal. Other original finishes include those mixed with different colored clays to produce a very light finish and terracotta that is tinted or striped. One attractive and popular terracotta finish is a solid black effect which can have either a sheen or be left matte. Stringently tested, it has been proven to be completely safe for use as tableware. This particular finish is achieved by firing normal terracotta, and while still hot covering it with rice husks, leaves and other vegetation. This burns into the surface turning it ebony black. A subtle sheen is achieved by rubbing coconut oil into the finished product.

▲ *Terracotta vases sprayed with tamarind juice. courtesy of Out of Asia*

◀ *Black terracotta tableware.*

▶ *The dappled look of terracotta sprayed with tamarind juice.*

Ceramic Production

There are many large manufacturers of ceramics in Indonesia whose importance to the export market must be recognized and respected. However, it is Jenggala and one or two other smaller producers who have set unprecedented high design standards for Indonesian ceramics.

Jenggala Keramik, set up in Bali in 1976, was the brainchild of New Zealand designer-potter Brent Hesslyn, Indonesian hotelier Wija Waworuntu and his daughter Ade. Using materials and production techniques quite unknown to local craftspeople, Jenggala began as a very small experimental cottage industry in Batu Jimbar, Sanur but in recent years moved production to Jimbaran. Jenggala produces ceramics of a standard comparable to countries with long histories of ceramic production. Their designs are a particularly fine example of the high quality of Indonesian craftsmanship.

▲   *Detail of ceramic teapots. courtesy of Jenggala*

▶   *Making a ceramic teapot.*

◀   *Ceramic cup, bowls and plate. courtesy of Jenggala*

▶▶   *Detail of ceramic plates. courtesy of Jenggala*

STONE

▲ *Bobos stone bathroom set. courtesy of Out of Asia*

◄ *Carving a stone relief in Bali.*

Striking evidence of Indonesia's creative stonework can be found in the stunning monuments and temple complexes spread throughout the country, particularly in Java and Bali. Perhaps the best known of these is Borobudur which was built in the 9th century and is located in Central Java. The walls of this Buddhist monument are lined with 1,460 intricately carved panels of reliefs depicting the life of Buddha. Other notable examples of the skill of Indonesian stone carvers of former days are Prambanan, a large Hindu temple also built in the 9th century, and the Majapahit temples of East Java dating back to the 13th century. These temples remain in relatively good condition (albeit with the help of considerable reconstruction work), having withstood the ravages of both man and nature over many centuries. This is because the material used in their construction is volcanic lava rock, a particularly strong variety of stone. With Indonesia's 151 active volcanoes – the most in the world – the supply of lava rock remains plentiful.

In Bali, local people still create stone carvings for their temples and other buildings, but in Java this ceased with the rising prominence of Islam from the 14th century onwards when mosques replaced temples as places of worship. Instead, Javanese stonecarvers tend to focus on making statuary: the roads approaching Borobudur are lined with shops selling stone-carved figures from the Ramayana and Mahabharata epics, Hindu deities, and Indonesian national heroes such as Diponegoro. Although these carvings from volcanic lava rock are sometimes of monumental size and questionable taste, they are nonetheless artistic and skillfully produced. Also found in these roadside stalls are everyday functional items – such as mortars, pestles and chopping boards – carved from the volcanic lava rock that is supplied by the nearby active volcano Mt. Merapi.

In Java there are also abundant resources of *palimanan* limestone. The original *palimanan* comes from West Java, from the village of Palimanan near Cirebon. *Palimanan* limestone is also found in the Gunung Kidul area, twenty-five kilometers from Yogyakarta. The town of Wonosobo, home to many stonecarvers, is also located nearby. Many thousands of years ago *palimanan* limestone was formed at the bottom of the

◀ *Black mahogany table with white stone and resin.*

▶ *Grey marble bathroom set with mahogany. courtesy of Out of Asia*

▲ *Wood stone vases, canister and tealights. courtesy of Out of Asia*

◀ *Detail of wood stone vases.*

sea, but it gradually rose above sea level due to continuing underwater activity, thus creating non-volcanic mountains such as Gunung Kidul. *Palimanan* comes in various colors and strengths dependent on the content of shells and other sea life. The strongest form is called *trotol* which is gray in color and usually has to be machine cut. This stone can be used to produce items in strong, sharp shapes. Other forms of *palimanan* are softer and come in various shades of cream and gray. Some forms of yellow *palimanan* are streaked brown, giving it a unique and attractive character. The most special of these is commonly called "wood stone". It is a rare variety of *palimanan*, harder and stronger with an interesting, mottled effect similar to a timber finish.

In Bali a much softer stone called *paras* is normally used in statuary and temple buildings. *Paras* is a sedimentary rock similar to sandstone and is sometimes referred to as volcanic tuff. The Balinese prefer to work in *paras* as it suits the intricacy of their stone-carvings. Most temples and other buildings in Bali use *paras* for decoration as actual parts of the structure such as undecorated walls. Compared to volcanic lava rock, *paras* has a shorter life span. As carvings and buildings made from *paras* are continually replaced, the tradition of stonecarving is ensured.

Along the streets of Balinese villages specializing in stone-carving, such as Batubulan in the region of Gianyar, one can see beautiful, intricately-carved statues and other decorative and functional objects ranging from large free-standing panels to water fountains made in yellow and grey *palimanan* and *paras*.

More recently, marble and onyx have become two of the most sought after types of stone used in the production of home accessories. Marble is an extremely durable and handsome material and because of this durability it is ideal for items used in the home on a daily basis. Examples include vases and kitchen and bathroom accessories where a combination of good looks and practicality are important. Marble also has a certain perceived value so it tends to be used in the production of more exclusive, high-end items. In the last five years the export of household items made from marble has almost quadrupled in line with an increasing overseas demand for this material. The color range of marble available in greater volume is limited to black, gray and cream but the quality is extremely high and superior to that from neighboring Southeast Asian countries. Onyx is used for more decorative items and is particularly popular with Asian buyers.

A derivative of marble is terrazzo. Originally used as a flooring material, it is formed by the combination of marble or granite chips set in concrete and then polished to a smooth finish. Terrazzo can be produced in a wide range of colors by the addition of pigments into the concrete. It is an ideal material for various items used outdoors such as garden pots and furniture. It is also widely used in practical, decorative items that are used indoors such as vases, lamp bases, or kitchen and bathroom accessories. A great advantage of terrazzo is that, unlike other stone products, it can be molded into desired shapes.

▲ *Terrazzo lamp, candle plates and containers with leather lids. courtesy of Out of Asia*

▶ *Onyx candle holders with mahogany bases. courtesy of Warwick Purser Lifestyle*

▲   *Black terrazzo bowl and
decorative ball.*

◀   *Grey* trotol *stone with chrome
finishing: vases, napkin ring,
canister, candle plates and candle
holder. courtesy of Out of Asia*

Compared to other materials, stone is particularly durable and therefore suited to functional items that are used on an everyday basis in the home, most especially in the bathroom and kitchen. Also, because there is a contemporary appearance about the material, it is ideal for accessories in modern homes. Bathroom items may include soap dishes, toothbrush, cotton bud or tissue box holders. For kitchen use, items made from marble include cheese cutters and cutting boards, to mention only a few. Flower vases of different shapes and sizes, decorative and functional bowls for salads and general tabletop use, stone candle holders, lamp bases and flower pots are all in great demand. Innovative designs combining marble, stone and wood result in beautiful pieces of furniture.

In comparison to the other materials mentioned in this volume, stone is much more difficult to work with and requires more specialized skills. Production is therefore slower and large orders for handmade stone items often need more time to complete. With the innate skills of Indonesia's stonecarvers and the wide variety of readily-available stone, it is no wonder that Indonesia is in the forefront of countries exporting household items handcrafted from this material and its man-made associates.

▲ *Mahogany bowls.*

◀ *Carving mirror frames in Bali.*

Indonesia possesses one of the world's largest resources of many important species of timber including teak, mahogany, *nyatoh* (which is similar in appearance to teak), *meranti* and *merbau*. Fortunately, much of this timber is now being grown in a sustainable manner in controlled plantations.

The tradition of carving in wood in Indonesia dates back many centuries. Throughout Indonesia one can find beautifully carved wooden pavilions, walls, doors and window frames that are important features of traditional architecture. In Bali, the carvings of decorative motifs and mythological figures found in housing and temples is particularly fine and intricate. Elsewhere, woodcarvings may incorporate designs ranging from the simple to the intricate, as well as the more primitive, dramatic designs from other regions of Indonesia such as Kalimantan, Lombok and Papua.

The very same skill traditionally required in the making of decorative woodcarving is also now employed in the crafting of beautiful home accessories such as candleholders, salad servers, rice spoons, lamp bases, and wooden bathroom accessories. In the production of wood items, machines are replacing hands but there are still many items that do require hands or at least a combination of machines and hands in their production.

In Indonesia – particularly Java – there is also an active furniture production industry. In many cases Indonesia produces furniture of a higher quality than its Asian neighbors that is eagerly sought by overseas retailers. Rather than focusing on markets that are looking for mass produced products, Indonesian craftspeople have come up with various strategies to ensure that they can be both competitive and innovative. Handcrafted wooden furniture items are a perfect example of this strategy. In Java and Bali there are many workshops producing beautiful handmade furniture of great quality which finds its way into a special niche market.

The production of specialty furniture includes one-off pieces such as modern day "antiques" using old timber – particularly teak – which gives the newly assembled item an appearance of considerable age. There is a lot of old teak in Indonesia that can be used in the production of these items.

▶ *6m long table made from aged teak. courtesy of Aulia*

◀ *Detail of aged teak table.*

In an attempt to be more innovative than their Asian competitors and to strengthen their position in the specialty furniture market, Indonesian craftspeople combine timber with other materials such as bamboo, natural fibers, resin and stone. Examples include wood frames for tabletops that are made of slatted bamboo, banana bark, granite, terrazzo or marble. A wooden cupboard may incorporate a panel of resin with an inlay of coconut shell, and wooden chairs are upholstered in woven pandanus.

▲ *and* ▶▶ *Handcarved wooden mirror frames. courtesy of I Made Astawa*

▶ *Woven coconut shell ice buckets and cabinet made from coconut shell and yellow sea penshell with wooden screen. courtesy of Carlo*

◀ *Detail of coconut shell cabinet.*

Household items from wood include salad bowls made of aged teak, serving plates created in *nyatoh* wood, and vases made from mahogany set with glass. Wood veneer is also starting to play an important role as a material used in the creation of household items. When applied to terracotta vases, plates or bowls, wood veneer gives the impression that the object is made of a solid piece of wood and therefore increases its perceived value. Another advantage of wood veneer is that it has greater acceptability to a market that is increasingly more aware of protecting the environment.

▲ *Teak veneer-covered terracotta vases and plate. courtesy of Out of Asia*

◀ *Detail of teak-covered terracotta vases.*

▶ *Ebony homeware collection embedded with* mendong *and* pandanus. *courtesy of Tropis*

▲ *Steel lamps. courtesy of Upnormal*

◀ *Welding steel in Bali.*

The ability to manufacture metal tools in Indonesia dates back to the prehistoric period, and this skill has developed until today. For over a thousand years, Indonesians have used iron, gold, silver, copper and bronze in jewelry, coinage, agricultural implements, weapons and home utensils.

Since at least the 9th century Indonesian blacksmiths have applied many techniques for the making of metal statuary, jewelry and household items, including forging, repoussé, chasing, engraving, raising, blocking, hollowing and lost wax. In the method of bronze casting known as "lost wax", a craftsman begins by modelling a wax figure or object, even using threads dipped in wax to add extra details. The figure is then ready for casting into bronze or other metals. To do this, the craftsman puts a clay cladding over the wax figure to create a negative mould. The molten metal is then poured into the clay mould which contains the wax figure. The heat of the metal melts the wax which then escapes through a small duct. The molten metal fills the space left by the wax and is allowed to cool and set inside the clay casing. The clay mould is then broken, revealing a metal statue or object.

Perhaps the skill of blacksmiths reached its peak with the production of the *kris* which is now more of a ceremonial sword

▲ *120cm long stainless steel door handles with a hairbrush finish. courtesy of Pintor Sirait*

◄ *Detail of door handle.*

although in former days it was a functional weapon. The *kris* is found throughout Indonesia, in Java, Sumatra, Kalimantan, Sulawesi, Maluku, Bali, West Nusa Tenggara and East Nusa Tenggara. The *kris* can also be found in other countries which were influenced by the Majapahit culture, such as Malaysia, Thailand, Cambodia, the Philippines and Brunei. In addition to being an heirloom and talisman, the *kris* is also an art object which encompasses the art of metal handiwork, carving, sculpting and shaping. The *kris* has always held an important position in Indonesian culture. A Javanese proverb states that a man cannot be considered "complete" without one, and this makes it one of the most highly valued objects in a Javanese household.

The metal used in a *kris* is a combination of iron, nickel, steel and sometimes gold. In Java a *kris* maker is called *empu* as a term of respect. As a blacksmith, the *empu* is considered to have special skills in the handling of iron and fire, and also to have magical powers. The *kris* is not just a handcrafted object but also a symbol of spiritual forces.

In Yogyakarta, the district of Kota Gede has a number of workshops producing jewelry, as well as silver and silver-plated objects. Kota Gede, founded in 1582, is the original capital of the great Muslim kingdom of Mataram, which controlled most of Java until the Dutch arrived. Some lasting impressions of the old city can be found in houses owned by the Kalang people who were woodcarvers and goldsmiths. Requested by the kingdom of Mataram to fulfill its need for artisans, they had originally come from the Hindu kingdom of Majapahit in East Java and Bali. Over time, because of the skill of their workmanship and their trading ability, many of the Kalang became very rich. This wealth is still evidenced in some of the huge houses that remain in this part of Yogyakarta. The Kalang built luxurious houses with Hindu Javanese architecture, and later in the 19th and 20th centuries they incorporated Javanese traditional architecture with a *musholla* (a small mosque), Arabic ornamentation, and even European Baroque architecture. During the 1920s-1930s, the Dutch colonial government granted monopolies to the Kalang to handle private pawnshops, diamond and opium trading.

Metal is often overlooked amongst the better-known materials used by Indonesian craftspeople in the production of handmade items for export but there are certainly many examples of beautiful Indonesian handcrafted products made in this material found in leading stores and galleries around the world. Rather than trying to compete with China and India in the export of mass-produced metal home accessories, Indonesia focuses on items such as jewelry that are more exclusive and aesthetically more beautiful.

▲ *Stainless steel coffee table. courtesy of Pintor Sirait*

▶ *Woven aluminum dining table. courtesy of Laurence Sanders*

◀ *Detail of woven aluminum mirror frame and lamp stand. courtesy of Laurence Sanders*

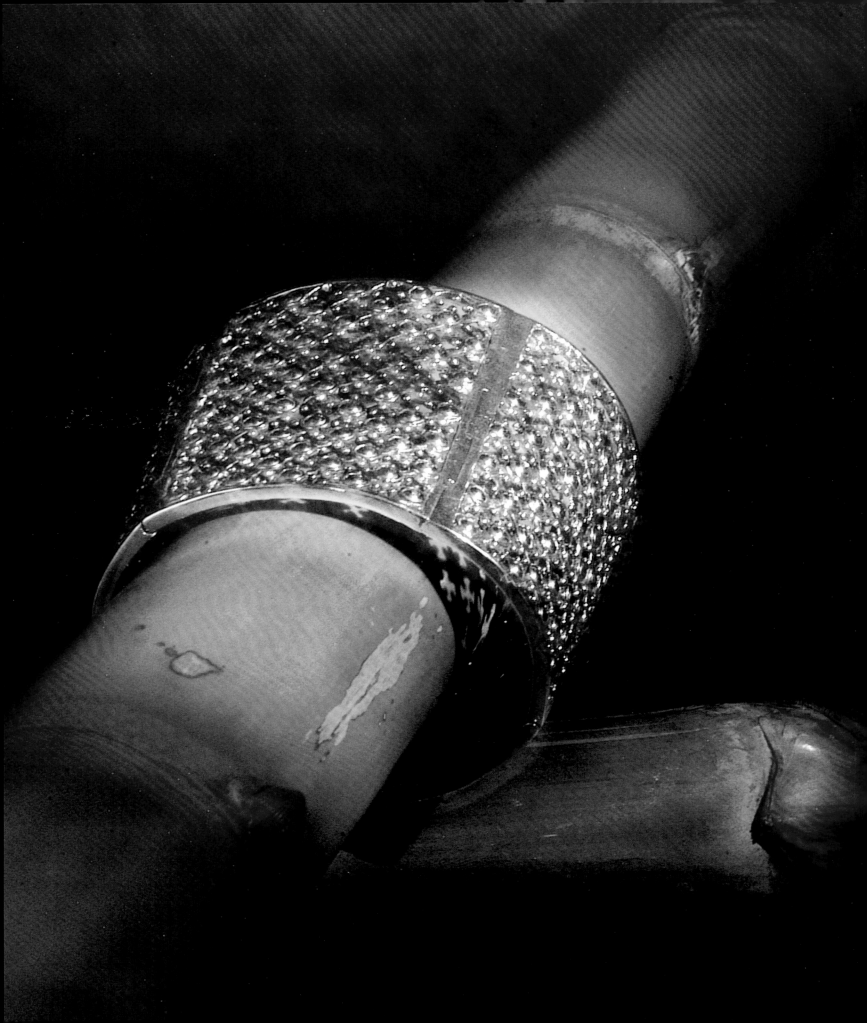

The Canadian jewelry designer John Hardy employs hundreds of skilled local craftspeople in his workshop in Bali. Of all the jewelry designers in Indonesia, he has perhaps made the greatest impact on the overseas jewelry market. Today John Hardy jewelry is found in the most sophisticated department stores of the world, including Neiman Marcus and Saks Fifth Avenue.

In Bali there are hundreds of gifted jewelry designers and manufacturers. If you take a trip along the main road of Celuk en route to Ubud, you will pass many workshops producing highly intricate, handmade jewelry items of all price ranges using materials such as aluminum, stainless steel, copper, silver, gold, galvanized metal (iron or steel coated with a protective layer of zinc), bronze (an alloy of copper and tin) and pewter (an alloy of tin, copper and antimony). Indonesian craftspeople also use these materials to produce non-jewelry items such as handcrafted bowls, vases, bathroom accessories and candlesticks.

▲ *Handcarved silver chain watch. courtesy of John Hardy*

◀ *Handmade "Jaisalmer" sterling silver and gold conical cuff. courtesy of John Hardy*

▶ *Chrysoprase cross pendant with diamonds. courtesy of John Hardy*

Throughout Indonesia, certain villages or districts specialize in the production of handcrafted items made from particular materials. In the case of metal, the established centers for silver production are Celuk in Bali and Kota Gede in Java. Production centers for items made from aluminum and stainless steel can be found in Solo in Central Java and Malang in East Java. The inhabitants of the village of Tumang Cepogo in Central Java are almost completely devoted to the production of items from copper. In South Sumatra, Bangka is home to one of the world's largest tin mines and it is becoming Indonesia's center of pewter production.

Indonesian craftspeople often combine different materials in the creation of home accessories. This is also the case with metal, where stainless steel is combined with leather to create picture frames and desk accessories; aluminum is combined with stone to produce bathroom accessories; silver is combined with coconut wood and bamboo to create beautiful decorative items for table settings as well as the metal handles and lids for various household items made from natural fibers.

▲   *Beaten copper bowls.*

▶   *Detail of beaten copper bowls.*

▲ *Detail of woven* agel *striped hatbox,* mendong *and cotton picture frame and napkin ring.*

◀ *Weaving* mendong.

▶▶ Agel *picture frame, laundry basket and tissue box,* mendong *boxes, placemat and napkin rings, painted water hyacinth container. courtesy of Out of Asia*

By far, the most widely used materials in the production of Indonesian craftwork are the natural fibers derived from indigenous plants. Products made with natural fibers have a distinct "made in Indonesia" look about them because in many cases the materials are unique to Indonesia.

These natural fibers are durable, sustainable and in many cases quite exotic. They range from the better known basics such as pandanus, rattan and vetiver (cedar root), to the less well known ones such as the stems of banana plants, water hyacinth, *mendong* (a type of grass), *agel* (a type of leaf), *lidi* (the spines of palm leaves), and *lontar* (palmyra palm leaves). They are already very beautiful in their natural form, but when they are woven into interesting shapes or used in combination with other materials, perhaps colored, and applied to the surface of various objects, they achieve another depth or an extension of their existence never imagined: vases covered with the "bark" of a banana plant stem, placemats woven with a combination of cotton and the spine of a coconut leaf, or storage boxes made from vetiver that have a fresh, tantalizing aroma.

Natural materials have long been used in construction and housing, and to create clothing and household items for daily use such as basketry and matting. Because of the very nature of these materials and the skill of the hands that create the various products using them, the forms have been easily adapted to the needs of the modern Western world. For example, a bamboo basket is transformed into a laundry container, or a pandanus floor mat is recreated into a place mat for the table. The total number of placemats from natural fibers that are exported annually is in excess of several million pieces. My company alone exported more than seven hundred thousand placemats last year.

There are very few natural fibers in Indonesia that in some way have not been incorporated into household items for export, and creative craftspeople are continually developing new ways to use these materials.

▲ *Handbags from woven* agel. *courtesy of CS Bags*

▶ *Woven pandanus bags, shoes and belt. courtesy of Miranda Shoes*

◀ *Handbags made from woven rattan, bamboo, leather,* mendong *and cotton. courtesy of CS Bags*

▲ *Woven pandanus charger plates, boxes and containers. courtesy of Out of Asia*

◄ *Detail of woven pandanus charger plates.*

▶ *Woven pandanus charger plate and dining chair. courtesy of Warwick Purser Lifestyle*

▶▶ *Woven pandanus laundry basket, containers, ottoman and placemat. courtesy of Warwick Purser Lifestyle*

Pandanus

Also known as *pandan* or screw pine, pandanus is a reed which grows throughout Indonesia, particularly on the island of Java. It is perhaps the most durable of all natural fibers and therefore the most popular. In Indonesia, pandanus was traditionally used in the production of large floor mats. The reed is harvested, cut, dried, in many cases colored, and then woven. In its natural loose form it is used for soft basketry but more often it may be applied to thick cardboard or plywood to form office and general living accessories for the home such as waste paper baskets, picture frames, and laundry baskets.

Pandanus that grows by the sea is tougher and harder to color and it is more appropriate in the production of furniture as well as baskets and storage containers. Pandanus growing on hillsides is softer and easier to color, and more suitable for smaller items such as storage boxes and trays. It can be dyed in a wide range of colors, which helps producers keep up with seasonal color trends.

Rattan

Rattan palm vines grow throughout the island of Kalimantan. Other types of rattan of a finer variety are found on the island of Lombok and islands further east. Rattan is commonly used in the production of furniture, and it is also used in the production of smaller items such as laundry and shopping baskets. It is particularly strong, but it does not take color as well as other natural fibers because it has a skin that prevents the dyes from being properly absorbed. Sometimes it is painted as an alternative to being dyed. Local supplies of this material are often disrupted because of the large amounts of rattan that are smuggled illegally out of Indonesia via Malaysia to China. The Indonesian government is now taking steps to stop this activity.

▲ *and* ◀ *Terracotta vases covered with rattan. courtesy of Out of Asia*

▶ *Detail of terracotta vase covered with rattan.*

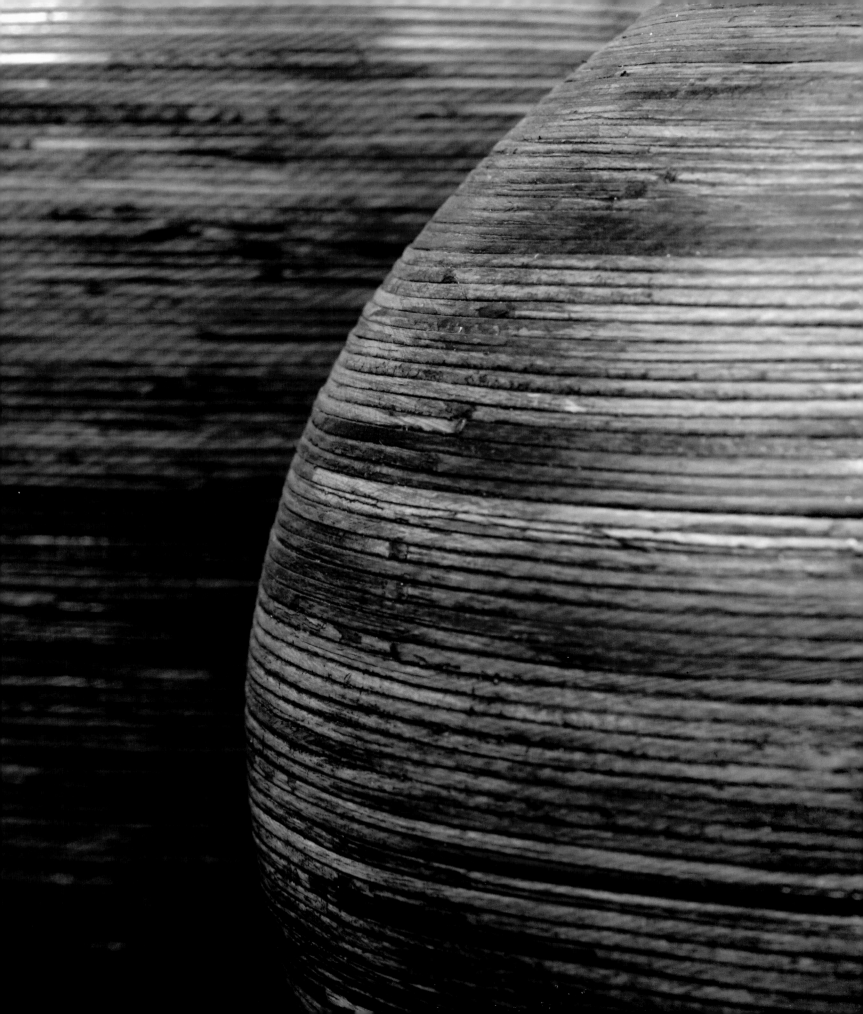

Terracotta vases covered with the stem of the banana plant. courtesy of Out of Asia

Detail of terracotta covered with the stem of the banana plant.

Woven banana plant sofa. courtesy of Warwick Purser Lifestyle

Terracotta covered in banana laminating. courtesy of Out of Asia

The Stem of the Banana Plant

There are many types of banana plants in Indonesia, but according to the Javanese the most suitable one for use in handcrafted products is the stem of the *pisang batu* (stone banana) plant because its color is dark and adaptable in application. The stem of the banana plant has a lot of moisture so it retains elasticity even after being dried. Durable, it can be twisted and woven to form sofas and chairs. "Bark" from the stems of the banana plant is also used extensively as coverage for such items as terracotta vases, wooden boxes and trays. A number of well-known international shops including Crate & Barrel in the US carry a range of items made from this material.

Water Hyacinth

One of the most attractive natural fibers is the stem of the water hyacinth, a plant that grows in the various waterways of Indonesia, especially in Java. The water hyacinth plant was brought into Indonesia from Thailand at the turn of the century and to a great extent has become a weed clogging up the rivers and preventing the free passage of water traffic. The stems of the water hyacinth are dried then woven. Because of its strength, it can be woven to produce furniture and all sorts of household items, particularly basketry. It can also be very finely shredded and dyed to produce packaging, placemats and table runners.

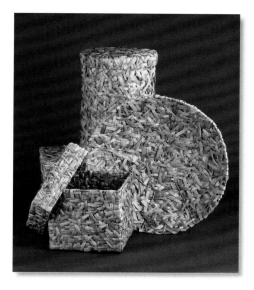

▲ *Water hyacinth laundry basket, box and large bowl. courtesy of Out of Asia*

◄ *Detail of water hyacinth laundry basket.*

▶ *Water hyacinth chair. courtesy of Warwick Purser Lifestyle*

▶▶ *Detail of finely-woven water hyacinth and cotton with screen printing.*

Mendong

A type of grass that grew on hillsides in the past, *mendong* was traditionally used in Indonesia as a material for woven floor mats. Now grown as a commercial crop, it is more often used to create storage boxes, sometimes in combination with other materials such as cardboard and plywood. It is a very soft fiber, easily woven together with cotton, and takes color quite well. After being colored it can be woven with plain colors to produce black and white checks or multicolored stripes.

Agel

A type of palm leaf, *agel* can be split into two parts. The lower part of the *agel* leaf is harder and tougher. The upper part is softer and can be dyed in a variety of colors including subtle, pastel tones. *Agel* can be finely shredded and woven with cotton to produce a very fine, sophisticated weave. Applied to the exterior of boxes, *agel* is particularly suitable for the packaging of items such as cosmetics. Both *mendong* and *agel* are used by Crabtree & Evelyn for the packaging of a number of their ranges.

▲ *Woven* mendong *and cotton hat box, picture frames, tissue box, wastebin, desk organizer and pencil pot. courtesy of Out of Asia*

▸ *Detail of woven* mendong.

◂ *Woven* agel *laundry basket, container, picture frame, tissue box and placemat. courtesy of Out of Asia*

▲ Lidi *console table, chair, picture frame, lamp, tray and hat box with mahogany. courtesy of Warwick Purser Lifestyle*

◄ *Detail of* lidi, *the stem of the coconut leaf.*

▶ *Woven vetiver pill box with cotton trim and table runner.*

Lidi

Lidi is the spine of the coconut leaf. In Indonesia, large bundles of these are tied together to form brooms. It is very tough, and has an attractive dark brown natural tone. *Lidi* is often used in combination with differently colored cottons to produce a variety of patterns for items ranging from placemats to large storage containers. One of America's largest retail chain stores claims that their latest best-selling item is a placemat made of this material. Over a two year period, they sold in excess of two hundred thousand pieces.

Vetiver

Traditionally, vetiver or cedar root was used on its own as a room or wardrobe freshener, especially in Java where it was important to keep batik cloths safe from moths and other insects. These days vetiver is woven in combination with thread or cotton to create placemats and many types of storage items. It is perhaps best known as the source for essential oil which is the base ingredient of a famous French perfume range of the same name.

Lontar

The *lontar* or palmyra palm is widely found in Bali and Lombok. The dried leaves can be written on, and were used traditionally in Indonesia in place of paper for writing. Thus the Indonesian word *lontar* is both the name for the palmyra palm tree, and a manuscript made of such palm leaves.

The leaves are strong and flexible so they can be woven into baskets and cushion covers. Palmyra palm leaves can also be applied to stiff board to make storage boxes.

In a world that seems to pay homage to everything synthetic, Indonesian handcrafted products created from natural fibers present the opportunity of living with and enjoying functional household items that are skillfully woven, beautifully colored, durable and sometimes naturally scented. The world is fortunate indeed that Indonesia has given them this alternative.

◄◄ *Woven* lontar *cushions, boxes, laundry basket and food covers. courtesy of Out of Asia*

▶ *Detail of* mendong

◄ *Woven* mendong *collection. courtesy of Out of Asia*

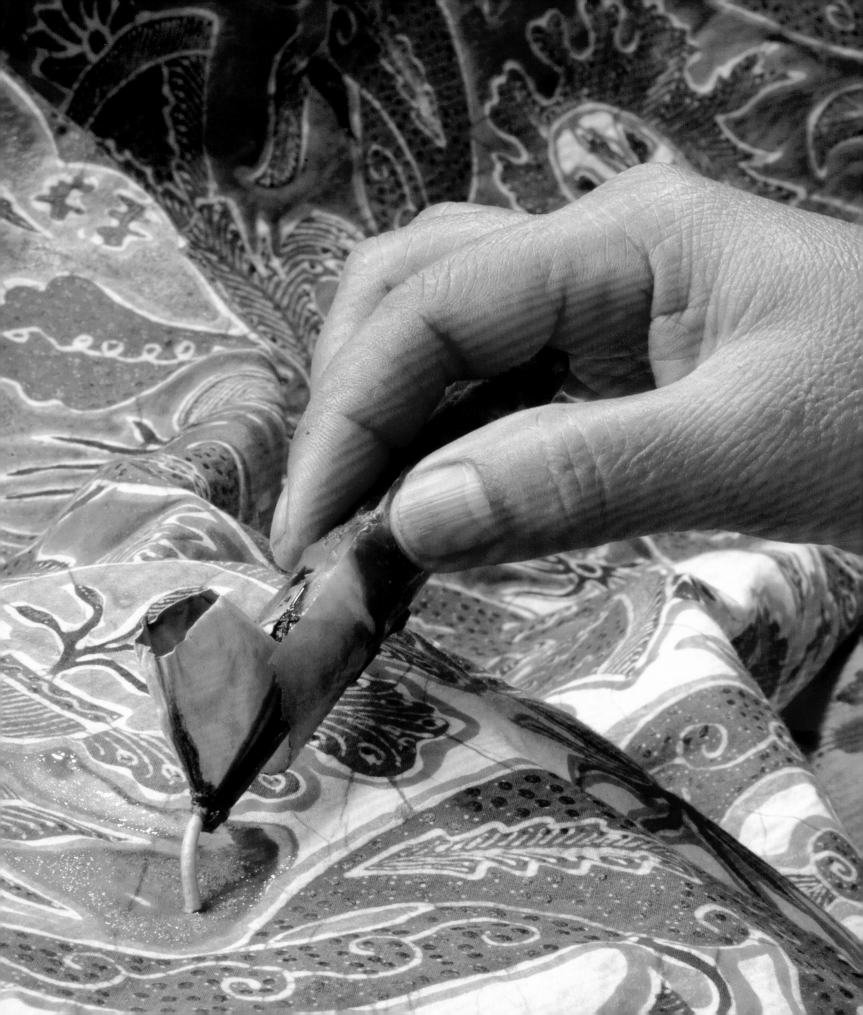

Embroidered, beaded and printed fabrics, ceramic dinner set. courtesy of Disini and Jenggala

◄ *Batik. courtesy of Ardiyanto*

Most people associate Indonesian textiles with batik. It is the most famous in a wide variety of Indonesian textiles and requires the most demanding skills for its production. As there have been many excellent publications on the subject of batik, the major emphasis in this chapter is other textiles exported from Indonesia, which are perhaps less well known.

Indonesia unquestionably remains the source of some of the world's most beautiful textiles – from the finest woven silk of South Sumatra and Sulawesi to the heavy *ikat* of eastern Indonesia and exquisite batik from Java. The Indonesian archipelago consists of more than five hundred widely spread ethnic groups which has resulted in a diversity of traditions. One of the typical cultural differences between the ethnic groups is the tradition of dressing. The manufacture of cloth by several Indonesian ethnic groups has become a distinctive skill in itself which has been handed down from generation to generation over the centuries. Apart from their use as clothing, these textiles had religious usage as a part of the sacred ceremonies of a particular ethnic group, and also to indicate the social status of the person who owned them.

▲ *Embroidered cushions. courtesy of Disini*

◀ *Printed and embroidered cotton cushions and pillows. courtesy of Disini*

Indonesian women and men still often wear beautifully woven textiles and batik, particularly if they are attending a ceremony of importance such as a wedding or funeral. At official and diplomatic receptions in Jakarta, it is common to see Indonesian women dressed in beautiful silks that are often heavily embroidered with gold and silver thread. Dressed in their traditional attire, they far outshine the overseas guests. At the same time, they are proud ambassadors for their country's textile industry.

This chapter is being written at a critical time for all those involved in the production and export of Indonesian textiles. Previously, to a certain extent the American quota system protected the textile industry of a number of developing countries. With the lifting of that quota system, China has now become the major player in the world arena of textile production. This change has certainly had a detrimental affect on the Indonesian textile business. A number of large factories have closed down, and some of the remaining factories have had to drastically reduce their work forces.

Indonesia relies on imports of raw cotton from the US, China and India. There are small mills in the city of Pekalongan and small communities in Troso and Jepara where the raw thread is spun by hand rather than by machine. However, the bulk of the raw cotton is spun in the large textile mills of Bandung in West Java. Unfortunately, many of these mills have now closed down as they were unable to compete with the cheaper spun cotton thread exported from China.

The argument that batik, for instance, is unique to Indonesia and therefore will not be affected by this new policy is not pertinent. Albeit in a limited capacity, China has now also started copying Indonesian batik designs and techniques. Of course, Indonesia has the competitive advantage in that hundred of years of tradition are not easy to duplicate and this is very much reflected in the fine quality of Indonesian batik design.

Batik cloth has been known since the 12th century. Initially originating from the island of Java, the major production centers for batik are now to be found in Pekalongan, Solo and Yogyakarta. Over the centuries, batik also began to be produced in Palembang, Bengkulu and Jambi in Sumatra. Technically, batik is a method of applying motifs onto cloth by the color-blocking dyeing process with the use of wax as the blocking medium.

The tradition of making beautiful textiles carries through into the modern age. Master designers such as Iwan Tirta and Josephine ("Obin") Komara ensure that batik and other traditional textiles remain relevant in the present. They continually develop modern, new designs and market their creations both at home and abroad. Obin in particular has extended her range beyond batik to exquisite handspun fabrics that are available in her own shops in Singapore and Japan and she is represented in other countries throughout the world. One piece of Obin's cloth can require as many as forty artisans to produce her distinctive look.

Modern batik garments and home accessories such as tablecloths, cushion covers, napkins and bedcovers often incorporate traditional designs and motifs but also these can be modified and the colors may be changed to meet fashion demands. Even so, much of the basic design still relies on traditional elements.

Traditional methods of weaving are still used, particularly on the islands of Lombok, Nias, Sumba and Sumbawa, where many weavers use the back loom technique. All fibers are spun, dyed and woven by hand.

Among the many methods of applying a variety of designs on textiles, the technique of *ikat* has been one of the most

▲ *Terracotta covered with batik. courtesy of Iwan Tirta*

▶ *Detail of Iwan Tirta's batik.*

▲ *Cotton* ikat. *courtesy of Flamboyan*

▶▶ *Hand-woven and hand-batiked silk with "Tirtonadi" weave. courtesy of BIN House*

▲ *Hand-woven and hand-batiked silk with "floating" weave. courtesy of BIN House*

◄ *A selection of hand-woven and hand-batiked silk cloth. courtesy of BIN House*

popular. *Ikat* is amongst the oldest techniques (8ᵗʰ to 2ⁿᵈ century BC) of designing specific shapes and natural colors on cloth. The process of dyeing the yarn is carried out before the yarn is stretched onto the weaving loom. The traditional manner of weaving *ikat* cloth was by making a number of strong knots in a bundle of yarn following a certain pattern, so that those parts of the yarn covered by the knots will not be affected by color during the dyeing process.

While *ikat* cloths were used as clothing in the past, Indonesian *ikat* weavers are now weaving fabrics that can be used for upholstery and other textile items for home use. Some areas have specific *ikat* design. Bali for instance is the home of a particular *ikat* weave that is 100% cotton but with a sheen resembling Thai silk.

In Indonesia the most popular textile items exported are home accessories, garments and embroidered items ranging from hand screen-printed and batik sarongs to cotton, woven items made up as cushion covers and blankets. Screen-printed batik clothing remains a popular export item but as is the case with other textile items, this is also beginning to suffer from tough competition with textiles produced in China. Rasmini Gardner in Bali has done more than most to popularize household items made from Indonesian textiles and exports her products all over the world.

Lower-quality copies made in countries where production methods are cheaper will soon inundate the lower and middle levels of the international textile market. However, Indonesia has a long tradition in the art of producing textiles of extraordinary quality, and these examples of Indonesian craftsmanship are the difficult ones to copy. In the future there is little doubt that what will finally survive and what will always uniquely represent Indonesia in the overseas export market are the finer, more expensive, woven and batik items.

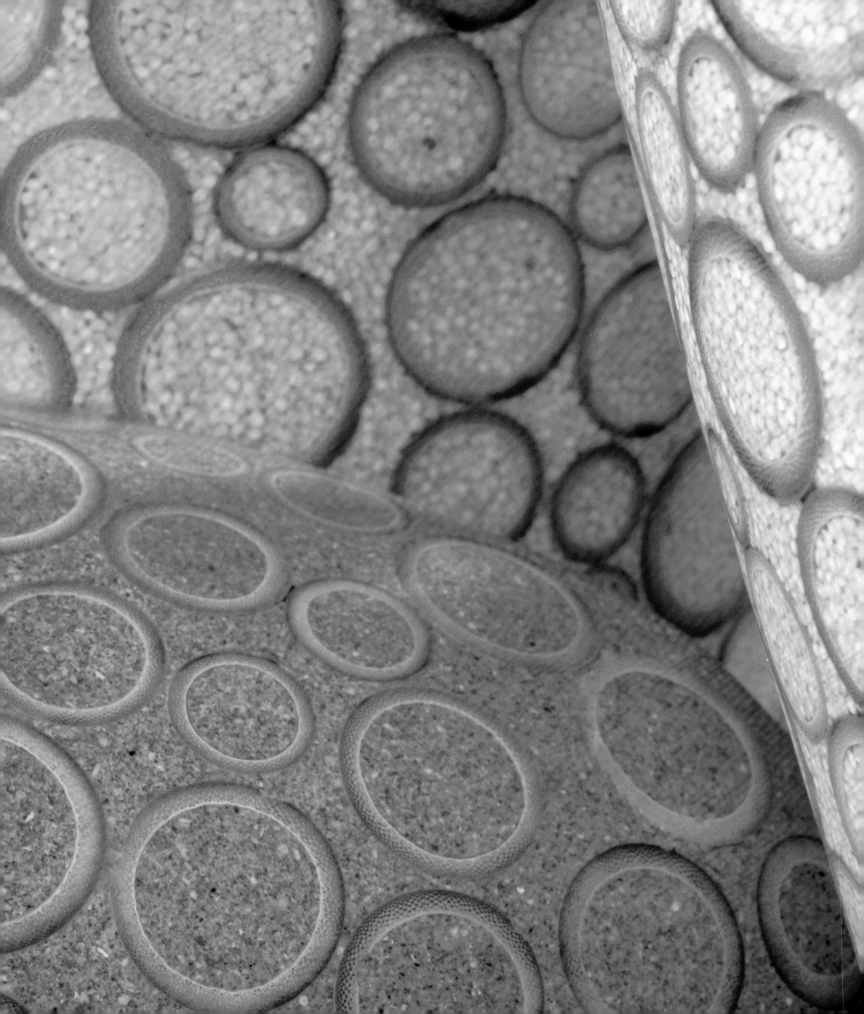

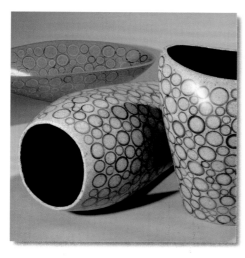

I am constantly amazed by the resourcefulness of Indonesian craftspeople to utilize materials that are not part of the standard repertoire. Take, for example, leaves and fern bark. While they are abundant throughout the country, who would have imagined that their application to other materials such as terracotta would lead to something distinctive and beautiful? Or who would have thought that you can make the most elegant of picture frames and tableware from the shells scattered across the miles of Indonesian beaches? This chapter explores some of the lesser-used materials like wax, resin, bamboo, leather and glass and the exclusive gallery-grade products that are created with this talent and resourcefulness.

▲ *Vases made of resin and birdseed with bamboo inlay, and bowl made of resin and sand with bamboo inlay. courtesy of Suka Koleksi.*

◀ *Detail of resin bowl and vases.*

▶ *Mother-of-pearl coasters, plates and bowls.*

Leaves and Fern Bark

Two of the most recent developments are leaves and fern bark applied to terracotta to give an interesting rustic finish. Although leaves from all types of trees can be used, the leaves of the mahogany and avocado trees are the most popular. The leaves are soaked in a solution of diluted chlorophyll to reduce the green color (which would otherwise fade), then dried and applied by glue to the surface of the terracotta. The leaves are then coated with a clear varnish.

Fern bark is another new application for terracotta and other solid materials. It is taken from fern trees which grow on mountainsides and continue to live and regenerate new bark. The bark is peeled, dried and then applied to a hard surface. After being applied it is cleaned with sand paper and sprayed with varnish. The finished item looks very much like an exotic plant.

▲ *Terracotta covered with fern bark. courtesy of Out of Asia*

▶ *Detail of terracotta covered with fern bark.*

▲ *Terracotta covered with leaves. courtesy of Out of Asia*

◀ *Detail of terracotta covered with leaves.*

Shell and resin picture frames, plates, decorative balls and salt and pepper shakers. courtesy of Out of Asia

◄ *Detail of shell and resin.*

▶ *Brown shell and resin picture frames, bowls, plate, decorative balls and salt and pepper shakers. courtesy of Out of Asia*

▶▶ *Detail of brown shell and resin.*

Shell

Shells of all types and varieties can be found on Indonesian beaches. In a country where beautiful, natural materials are usually incorporated into items for contemporary living, so it is with these offerings from the depths of the Indian Ocean.

Shells take on a new dimension when they are embedded into resin, set into wood or framed in silver and other metals. Some of the attractive handcrafted items incorporating shells include picture frames, mirrors, vases, sophisticated dining table accessories, candleholders and jewelry.

Mother of pearl is the most popular of all shell materials being used in the production of items for export, and is found in vast quantities on beaches throughout Indonesia – particularly those of the eastern islands. In its whole form as an unbroken shell it is often rimmed in silver to form beautiful containers. Depending on the size of the shell, it is possible to create small containers for salt and pepper or larger ones for sauces and other food dressings.

More often the shells are cut into round or square shapes and then set in resin to form tabletops, picture frames, trays and other decorative accessories.

Leather

While Indonesia has exported leather shoes, bags and jackets for some decades, only in the past few years have local craftspeople developed leather items with enough quality and creativity to attract the interest of international fashion labels. For example, Polo Ralph Lauren has recently begun sourcing storage boxes here, and several other brands have placed orders for leather picture frames, magazine holders, waste bins and desk accessories.

In other countries, large amounts of pigskin leather are used but in Indonesia leather is primarily sourced from cattle and goats. The skins are normally purchased directly from the abattoirs. Leather from the tanners comes in a natural brown color but, with the addition of pigment, it can be colored to match the demands of a buying market following the color trends dictated by the fashion industry. In the year that follows the launching of a new fashion collection, these trends have great impact on the colors and styles utilized in interior design products throughout the world.

▲ *Woven leather dining chair.*

▶ *Detail of leather boxes and picture frames.*

◀ *Leather waste bin, picture frame, magazine holder, tray, boxes and containers. courtesy of Out of Asia*

Handblown chiseled glass vase by Seiki Torige. courtesy of Galeri Esok Lusa

◀ *Glass art by Seiki Torige. courtesy of Galeri Esok Lusa*

▶ *Sandblasted latticed glass by Seiki Torige. courtesy of Galeri Esok Lusa*

▶▶ *Detail of latticed glass.*

Glass

Throughout the Kuta, Legian and Seminyak areas in Bali, many shops sell beautiful and unique handcrafted glassware. The pioneer artist in this medium was a Japanese named Seiki Torige who set up his kilns on an inaccessible beach in the region of Gianyar. His designs were noted for their sophistication and minimalism. His presence in Bali provided the stimulation for many local craftsmen to become glass artists, and many of his designs have been copied by local craftspeople.

Now available in greater quantities, handmade drinking glasses, plates and vases have now supplemented the magnificent one-off pieces of glass art. It would be wrong to say they are mass-produced because production techniques limit the quantities of each item. While Indonesia does have some very large factories using machines rather than hands concentrating on mass-production, the most talented of Indonesian craftspeople working with glass have chosen to concentrate on a particular niche market rather than try to enter the demanding mass market.

Resin

Resin has become a popular base component in the creation of interior homewares particularly in the Philippines, Thailand and more recently Indonesia. Many of Indonesia's handcrafted products have a rather rustic appearance but, when set in resin, their appearance changes to a slick, polished, minimalist look more suitable for contemporary design. This is most apparent in vases, tabletops, lamps, serving plates, mirrors, picture frames and even women's accessories made from this material. Of the many natural materials that are combined with resin to produce these items, bamboo and coconut shell are the most popular but others include cinnamon sticks and birdseed.

▲ *Cinnamon and resin lamp, picture frame and decorative balls. courtesy of Out of Asia*

▶ *Detail of cinnamon and resin.*

◀ *Cinnamon and resin shoes and handbag. courtesy of Miranda Shoes*

Italian designer Roberto Tenace of Produs Trend has been living in Bali for five years but he has used Bali as his design base since 1990. He has produced Indonesia's most beautiful range of household items using resin. From tall standing lamps to smaller serving plates with embedded dried leaves, his craft exemplifies the finest examples of what can be created using resin.

Although the relative amount in volume is less than other exports, resin-based products make a very significant impact to the overall high standard of design and creativity of Indonesian handcrafted products.

▲ *Resin lamps inlaid with leaves and seeds alongside bamboo and resin vases. courtesy of Produs Trend*

◄ *Detail of resin lamps.*

▶ *Dyed bamboo vases with resin inlay. courtesy of Produs Trend*

Materials such as glass and resin were not used in traditional Indonesian crafts, but they have been quickly taken up by local craftspeople. It often happens that expatriate designers and producers take the lead in introducing these materials to Indonesia and teaching the necessary skills that have to be applied in their production. However, considerable credit also has to be given to the local craftspeople for the speed with which they are able to adapt to something quite foreign to them. Indonesian craftspeople now produce items of great beauty in glass, resin, wax and other new media ranging from one-off pieces through to the mass production quantities applicable to the needs of large retailers.

▲ *Lotus flower cube, pillar, tapered and floating candles. courtesy of Sinar Alami*

◀ *Hammered textured cube, pillar and lantern candles. courtesy of Sinar Alami*

▶ *Painting a lotus candle. courtesy of Sinar Alami*

▲ *Bamboo and resin placemats, picture frame, vase, coasters and salt and pepper shakers. courtesy of Out of Asia*

▶▶ *Detail of bamboo and resin placemats.*

◀ *Bamboo and resin plates, picture frames, vases and decorative balls. courtesy of Suka Koleksi*

Bamboo

Bamboo is a material that has long been used in general construction as well as functional household items. There are many varieties of bamboo in Indonesia. In addition to the well-known natural yellow tone, bamboo is available in a dark brown color (commonly called "black bamboo") and there is also a speckled bamboo. All sorts of items ranging from placemats, trays, storage containers, waste bins, laundry baskets and furniture are made from this material.

There is also a very fine bamboo grown on the slopes of Mt. Merapi in Central Java, commonly called "bamboo *Chinois*" because it was widely used in the era of *Chinois* furniture which was at that time produced in China. The Japanese introduced "bamboo *Chinois*" into Indonesia in the 1940s. It is used extensively as an additional element to all sorts of different products including furniture, picture frames, boxes and bath towel racks.

One of the great advantages of bamboo is its sustainability. I remember one occasion when the amount required in producing a particular order was rather overwhelming, and this question of sustainability became a major issue. This happened seven years ago when my company had to produce half a million bamboo baskets for Body Shop packaging. Keeping in mind the necessity of continued sustainability, we decided to spread production over many centers rather than taking the easy step of centralizing production and relying on one source of supply. We did this so that the availability of the raw material would not be disrupted for the local peoples' daily use.

When one thinks of bamboo in Indonesia, one of the names that is immediately mentioned is Linda Garland. Not only did Linda spearhead the design of furniture and homeware using bamboo, she also founded the Environmental Bamboo Foundation in Bali in 1993 to develop the use of bamboo as a renewable non-wood forest resource. Linda has successfully shown that bamboo can be used for a wide range of products from flooring to jewelry, and has done much to promote bamboo as an alternative material to much less sustainable types of timber.

While the materials mentioned in this chapter are not amongst the major players in terms of what is produced for export, their addition ensures that Indonesia's range of items for export are amongst the most comprehensive in the world.

▲ *Bamboo and silver napkin ring. courtesy of Linda Garland*

▸ *Silver and bamboo bowls. courtesy of John Hardy*

◀ *Bamboo and shell tassel, bamboo and wood table, giant bamboo vase. courtesy of Linda Garland*

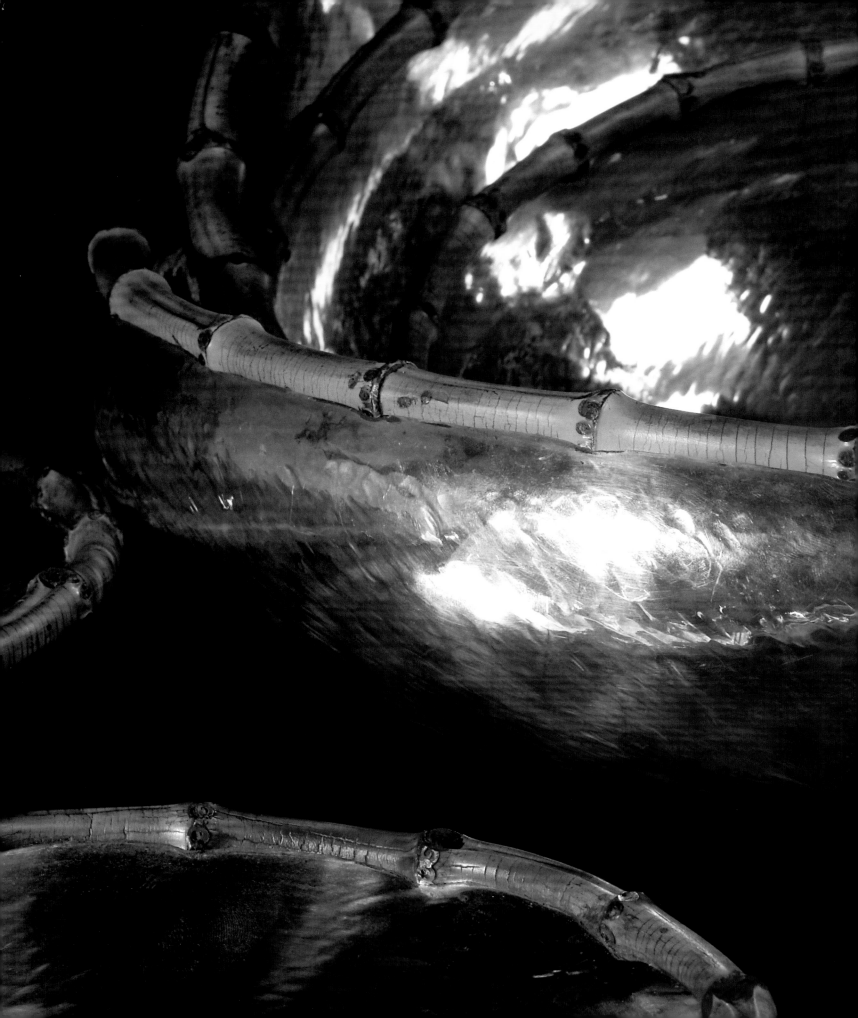

▲ *Woven recycled newspaper picture frame, placemat, pencil pot and desk organizer. courtesy of Out of Asia*

◀ *Detail of woven recycled newspaper and cotton.*

Perhaps the best evidence of the skill of Indonesia's craftspeople is the way in which they have taken everyday waste materials and transformed them into objects of great beauty and practicality with remarkable ingenuity. Significantly, this skill also makes a contribution to the protection of the environment.

With a population of 238 million people, domestic garbage alone is a huge environmental hazard in Indonesia. For example, there are 80,000 tons of flexible plastic packaging and 50,000 tons of propylene packaging produced each year. Like big cities elsewhere in the world, Jakarta yields tons of garbage every day. At no cost to the city, the processing of garbage is aided by the informal sector of trash pickers and scavengers called *pemulung*, an underpaid and marginalized sector of society. These people survive by collecting and reselling consumer waste. It is estimated that a group of fifty scavengers can gather a ton of garbage per month. Paper, plastic, wood, broken glass, plastic food and drink containers must all be sorted and bundled. Every week, the garbage is weighed and sold. From this garbage, certain materials are selected for the recycling process and they are later given new lives in the form of handcrafted objects.

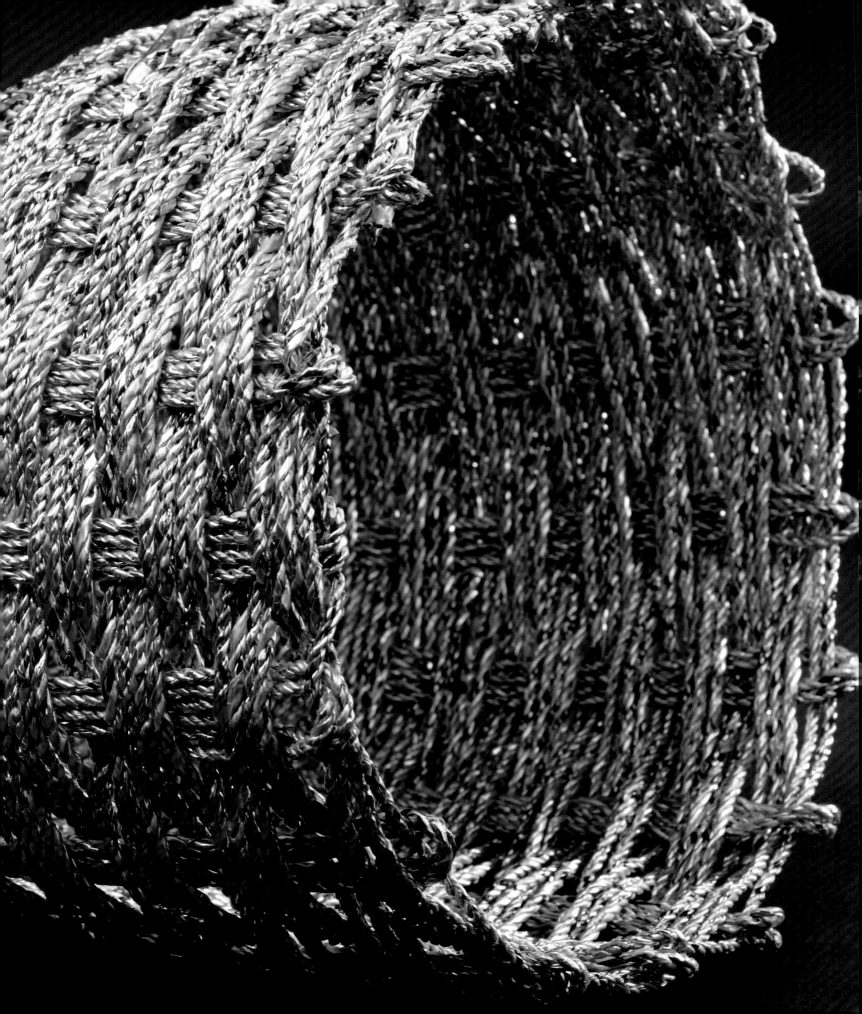

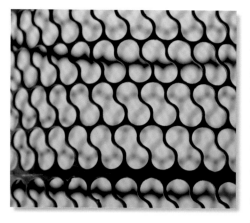

Indonesia's craftspeople continually discover new outlets for their talents. Using recycled materials of the most bizarre and humble nature, they transform and recreate them into handmade products of great beauty. It seems that nothing is beyond their imagination and their ability. Using simple equipment such as wooden looms and tin cutters, the recycled waste material is often woven or assembled onto cardboard, and sometimes welded. In these processes, the most important factors are the skills and ingenuity of the craftspeople who produce them.

▲ *Detail of recycled bicycle chain pen holder.*

◀ *Basket made from woven recycled chocolate bar wrappers. courtesy of Out of Asia*

▶ *Recycled bicycle chain desk set. courtesy of Out of Asia*

▶▶ *Recycled magazines woven with cotton collection. courtesy of Out of Asia*

Peacock made from recycled aluminum drink cans. courtesy of Out of Asia

Detail of woven recycled magazines.

Given time and a skilled pair of hands, one hundred and twenty-four used soft drink cans evolve into a metallic silver and green peacock which will later sit proudly on the reception desk of a luxurious international hotel in China. Carefully hand-twisted newspaper woven with cotton forms the basis of office containers for a leading US retail chain specializing in storage items. A container made with the leftover metal from the manufacture of bicycle chains now holds potpourri and is sold in internationally-known specialty stores in Europe. Smart, colorful bags made from recycled magazines can be found in boutiques in the south of France, and storage containers and bags made from the leftover woven plastic straps that were used to fasten cartons are found in shops throughout Europe.

Handcrafted objects made from recycled materials are not in any way "second-class citizens". They present a greater challenge in the art of their making when compared to handcrafted objects of a more "traditional" nature. Furthermore, they tend to have a contemporary look and feel to them.

If one had to choose the very best examples of the creative skill of Indonesia's craftspeople, there are probably none better than those made from recycled materials. Most importantly, through the process of recycling industrial "leftovers" and domestic garbage, they play a very important role in protecting Indonesia's environment. The challenge for the future is to find more and more ways in which leftovers and garbage can be recycled and re-used in the creation of handcrafted products. With the motivation of protecting the environment coupled with Indonesian creativity, undoubtedly more and more ways of doing this will be discovered.

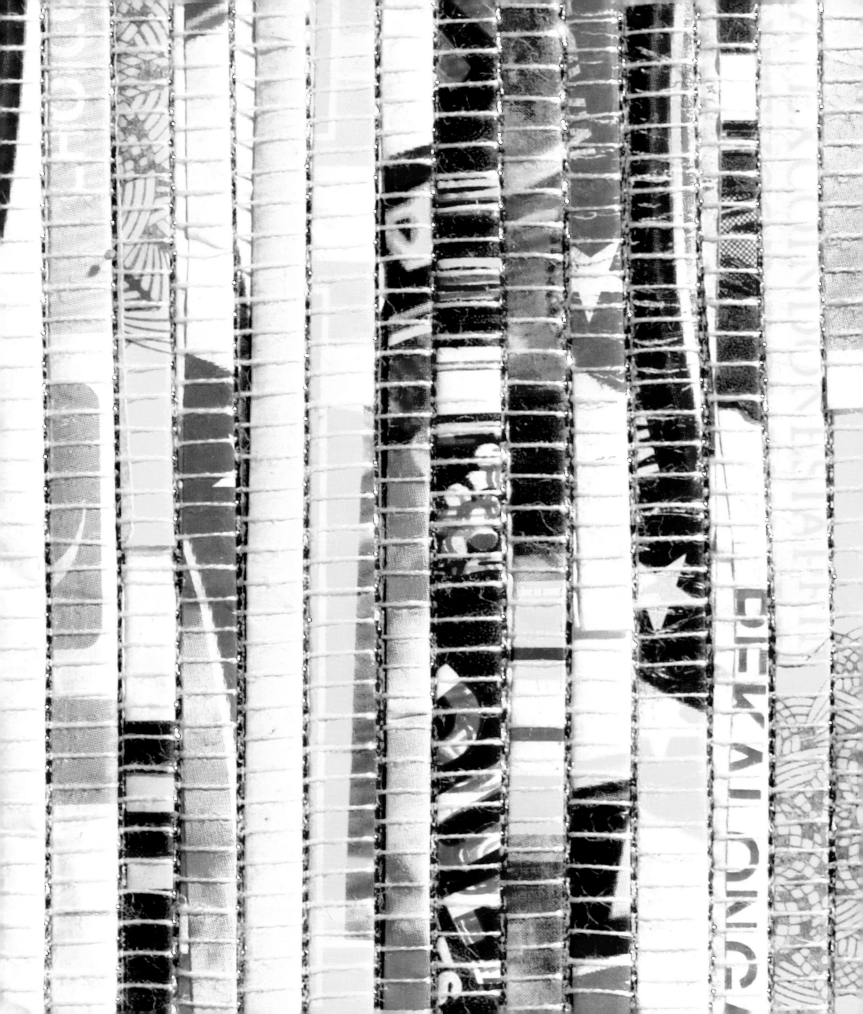

note: photos are in **bold**

GLOSSARY OF MATERIALS

 **Pandanus** (*Pandanus tectorius*) or screw pine is a small tree that grows up to 6m high. Its leaves are usually 90-150cm long and 5-7cm wide with saw-like edges. In loose form it is used for basketry, but can be applied to cardboard or plywood for picture frames and hampers.

 **Rattan** (from the Indonesian *rotan*), is the name for the roughly six hundred species of the genera *Calamus* and *Daemonorops* used for furniture and baskets. While very similar to bamboo, rattan is distinct in that it is solid rather than hollow, and also in their need for some sort of support – while bamboo can grow on its own, rattan cannot.

 ***Pisang batu*** (*Musa balbisiana*) or stone banana grows up to more than 6 metres high, and its stem can be twisted and woven to make furniture. Its bark can be colored and is used as coverage for terracotta and wooden household items.

 **Water Hyacinth** (*Eichhornia crassipes*) is one of the fastest growing plants known and can double its population in two weeks. The stems are dried and woven to produce goods ranging from furniture to baskets.

Mendong (*Fimbristylis globulosa*) is a type of grass indigenous to Java, Kalimantan and Bali and is common in secondary and primary forests. woven and colored is it ideal for storage boxes.

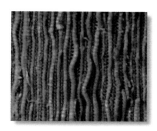

Vetiver (*Vetiveria zizanoides*) or cedar root is a tall, dense, wild grass with long narrow leaves and a strand of underground white, yellow and brown roots. It is most commonly known for its essential oil that reportedly has calming and soothing characteristics. In handcrafted products, vetiver can be woven with cotton for baskets or placemats.

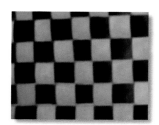

Lontar (*Borassus flabellifer*) or palmyra palm is a large tree up to 30m high and whose leaves are leathery, gray green, fan-shaped, 1-3m wide and folded along the midrib. The dried leaves can be woven to make numerous household items.

Lidi is the spine of the coconut plam leaf. In Indonesia, large bundles of these are tied together to form brooms. It is very tough, and has an attractive dark brown natural tone. *Lidi* is often used in combination with differently colored cottons to produce a variety of patterns to create placemats or large storage containers.

Agel (*Corypha utan*) is a type of palm leaf and can be split into two parts. The lower part of the *agel* leaf is harder and tougher. The upper part is softer and can be dyed in a variety of colors including subtle, pastel tones. *Agel* can be shredded and woven with cotton to produce a very fine weave.

LIST OF MANUFACTURERS

Although this book has been written by the founder and president of Out of Asia, we have attempted to include as many other manufacturers of handcrafted products as possible. The general rules for inclusion in this volume are
1. The products and raw materials must be made in Indonesia and by Indonesians,
2. The suppliers must consistently export their goods to reputable retailers worldwide, and
3. They must be able to accept quantity orders and deliver in good condition.
Those producers that meet these requirements are listed below. This list is not exhaustive as there are many more producers that we did not include in this book due to time and capacity restraints. We hope to include them in the next edition. All the information below was correct at the time of publication.

Ardiyanto Gallery
Jl. Magelang Km. 8
Yogyakarta 55285
T +62 274 562 777
F +62 274 563 280
E ardiyan@idola.net.id

Aulia Furniture
Jl Gunung Tangkuban Perahu No. 33X
Br. Padang Sumbu Tengah
Kerobokan, Kuta
Bali
T +62 361 742 8297
F +62 361 732 479
E aulia_furniture@yahoo.com

BIN House
Jl. Teluk Betung 10
Jakarta 10310
T +62 21 319 35941
F +62 21 315 2493
E info@binhouse.com
W www.binhouse.com

Carlo Showroom
Jl. Danau Poso No. 22
Sanur
Denpasar
Bali 80228
T +62 361 285 211
F +62 361 281 923
E info@carloshowroom.com
W www.carloshowroom.com

CS Bags
Adira Building
Jl. Magelang No. 77 (Km.7)
Yogyakarta 55285
T +62 274 748 9860
F +62 274 869 252
E info@csbags.net
W www.csbags.net

Disini
Jl. Raya Seminyak No. 6-8
Basangkasa, Seminyak, Kuta
Bali
T +62 361 731 037-763 715
F +62 361 764 887
E disini_bali@yahoo.com

Flamboyan Ltd.
Jl. Sekuta 23
Sanur
Bali 80228
T +62 361 287 220
F +62 361 289 952
E flamboyan@flamboyan.biz
W www.flamboyan.biz

I Made Astawa Wood Carvings
Jl. Raya Tegallalang-Kintamani Km.18
Bilukan-Sebatu, Tegallalang
Gianyar
Bali 80561
T +62 361 901 051
F +62 361 901 051

Iwan Tirta
Jl. Panarukan 25
Jakarta 10310
T +62 21 314 3122
F +62 21 3193 7244

Jenggala Keramik
Jl. Uluwatu II
Jimbaran
Bali
T +62 361 703 311
F +62 361 703 312
E info@jenggala-bali.com
W www.jenggala-bali.com

John Hardy
Jl. Baturning No. 1
Mambal
Denpasar
Bali
T +62 361 469 888
F +62 361 469 898
E john@johnhardy.com
W www.johnhardy.com

Laurence Sanders
Jl. Legian Kaje No. 2
Kuta
Bali
T +62 361 755 043
F +62 361 756 680
E laurencesanders@sandsbali.com
W www.sandsbali.com

Linda Garland Interior Design
Nyuh Kuning
Bali
T +62 361 974 028
F +62 361 974 029
E info@lindagarland.com
W www.lindagarland.com

Miranda Shoes
Jl. Hang Tuah 43
Sanur
Denpasar
Bali 80227
T +62 361 283 402
F +62 361 286 132
E info@mirandashoes.com
W www.mirandashoes.com

Out of Asia
Jl. Parangtritis Km 8.5
Tembi
Yogyakarta
T +62 274 368 250
F +62 274 368 281
E info@outofasia.co.id
W www.outofasia.co.id

Pintor Sirait
Jl. Mertasari 151
Suwung Kangin, Sanur
Bali
T +62 361 727 952
F +62 361 285 479
E info@pintorsirait.com
W www.pintorsirait.com

Produs Trend
Jl. Gunung Tangkuban Perahu No.1
Padang Sumbu, Padang Sambian, Klod
Denpasar
Bali
T +62 361 736 461
F +62 361 731 939
E trend777@telkom.net

Seiki Torige
c/o Galeri Esok Lusa
Jl. Raya Basangkasa No. 47
Seminyak, Kuta
Bali 80361
T +62 361 735 262
F +62 361 735 262
E info@esoklusa.com
W www.esoklusa.com

Sinar Alami
Jl. Ngurah Rai Bypass No. 144
Padang Galak, Sanur
Denpasar
Bali 80227
T +62 361 288 072
F +62 361 283 083
E info@sinaralami.com
W www.sinaralami.com

Suka Koleksi
Jl. Buana Raya No. 35
Padang Sambian
Denpasar
Bali 80117
T +62 361 486 829
F +62 361 486 830
E info@sukakoleksi.com
W www.sukakoleksi.com

Tropis
Gudang Bulog No.5
Jl. Uluwatu II
Jimbaran
Bali
T +62 361 742 6276
F +62 361 702 118
E info@tropisequator.com
W www.tropisequator.om

Upnormal
Jl. Raya Gunung Salak Utara No. 98
Kuta Utara
Denpasar
Bali
T +62 361 742 1970
F +62 361 414 700
E upnormalchen@yahoo.com

Warwick Purser Lifestyle
Jl. Kemang Raya 37A
Jakarta 12730
T +62 21 719 3317
F +62 21 719 5541
E info@warwickpurser.com
W www.warwickpurser.com

ACKNOWLEDGEMENTS

Although this book had been a dream for a few years it became a reality in a few days. The process of the reality started with a request to me from Mrs. Tatty Bakrie, wife of our Coordinating Minister for the Economy Aburizal Bakrie, to make the Minister's official residence into a showcase for Indonesian furniture, interior accessories and art. This venue was scheduled to be used by Mrs. Bakrie to host a morning event to be attended by Mrs. Susilo Bambang Yudhoyono, the wife of our President, other minister's and foreign ambassador's wives in her effort to promote Indonesian handcrafted products. This seemed such an ideal event to launch my much dreamed about book on that very same subject.

Mrs. Bakrie quickly confirmed she would head a committee to seek sponsors we identified a potential publisher in Mark Hanusz of Equinox. The first person I approached to join this committee and perhaps be one of those sponsors was my friend Richard McHowat, CEO of HSBC. After explaining the objective of the book and outlining what it might cost, I asked if HSBC would consider being a sponsor. I remember so clearly his reply: "Indonesia needs such a publication. HSBC won't be *a* sponsor, it will be *the* sponsor." After this, the services of Rio Helmi, Indonesia's brilliant photographer, and those of my daughter Polly as stylist were quickly confirmed and with the blessing of the Coordinating Minister for the Economy and the support of his wife – years of dreaming were realized in days.

If those people already mentioned were the star players the supporting cast was equally as supportive and enthusiastic: Mrs. Itjih Nursalim and Cherie Nursalim whose love and understanding of Indonesian handcrafted products is deep and sincere; my original partner in Out of Asia, Lesley Ho; Tience Sumartini, Eva Riyanti Hutapea and Maria Lukito of the Indonesian Chamber of Commerce; Miranda Goeltom of Bank Indonesia who not unsurprisingly has such an intelligent understanding of this business; dear friends and colleagues Rasmini Gardner and Peter Machin; Feraldi W. Loeis & Louise von Monk from the IFC project in Bali who are experts in the field of export of handcrafted people and who offered such good practical advice during the writing of the book: Peter Craven and my wonderful staff from Out of Asia in particular Ignast and Mulyadi for their help with background information for the text; Ririn, Sukir and Ries whose tolerance, dedication and help was enormous and who all made a huge contribution; Mendez who, most importantly, made sure everyone was so well fed throughout the duration of the project. One of most wonderful things about this book was the sense of teamwork from beginning to end – and to that very special team I give my heartfelt thanks.

Thanks to Mrs. Tatty Aburizal Bakrie for your continued involvement and support; Richard McHowat who apart from being the main sponsor also gave valuable input into the book's content; Mark Hanusz for all your enthusiasm and professionalism; Rio Helmi whose photographs bear witness to your great talent; Polly Purser who made everything in the pages of this book look so beautiful; Michelle Chin who had the challenging task of editing the output of this inexperienced writer; and Peter Hogg for his clear and concise proofreading.

There are a multitude of people with a long standing association with Indonesia who, over the years, have helped open both my eyes and those of many others to the beautiful handcrafted products of this country: Sergo dello Strologo who sadly is no longer with us and who set up Indonesia's first comprehensive display of Indonesian handcrafts in the late 70's at the Sarinah Department Store; Linda Garland who once paid me the great complement of saying I had taken over where she had left off; Lisa Purser who helped so much to develop my sensitivity to the beauty of natural materials in this country, Gabriella Teggia, Kerry and Ruth Hill, Peter & Carol Muller and Made Wijaya to name a few of those who have been close to me for many years and who have helped create so much beauty in this country in varying forms – be it architecture, landscape gardening or others.

And of course the people who deserve the most appreciation – the people who really made this book possible – the wonderful creative craftspeople of Indonesia. May this book show the world what great talent you have and how deserving you are of a publication that pays tribute to this talent.

also from EQUINOX PUBLISHING

NON-FICTION

THE SECOND FRONT:
Inside Asia's Most
Dangerous
Terrorist Network
Ken Conboy
979-3780-09-6
2005, softcover, 256 pages

WARS WITHIN:
The Story of TEMPO,
an Independent Magazine
in Soeharto's Indonesia
Janet Steele
979-3780-08-8
2005, softcover, 368 pages

SIDELINES:
Thought Pieces from
TEMPO Magazine
Goenawan Mohamad
979-3780-07-X
2005, softcover, 260 pages

AN ENDLESS JOURNEY:
Reflections of an
Indonesian Journalist
Herawati Diah
979-3780-06-1
2005, softcover, 304 pages

SRIRO'S DESK REFERENCE
OF INDONESIAN LAW 2005
Andrew I. Sriro
979-3780-03-7
2005, softcover, 200 pages

BULE GILA:
Tales of a Dutch Barman
in Jakarta
Bartele Santema
979-3780-04-5
2005, softcover, 160 pages

THE INVISIBLE PALACE:
The True Story of a
Journalist's Murder in Java
José Manuel Tesoro
979-97964-7-4
2004, softcover, 328 pages

INTEL:
Inside Indonesia's
Intelligence Service
Ken Conboy
979-97964-4-X
2004, softcover, 264 pages

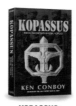

KOPASSUS:
Inside Indonesia's
Special Forces
Ken Conboy
979-95898-8-6
2003, softcover, 352 pages

TIMOR: A Nation Reborn
Bill Nicol
979-95898-6-X
2002, softcover, 352 pages

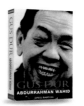

GUS DUR:
The Authorized Biography of
Abdurrahman Wahid
Greg Barton
979-95898-5-1
2002, softcover, 436 pages

NO REGRETS:
Reflections of a
Presidential Spokesman
Wimar Witoelar
979-95898-4-3
2002, softcover, 200 pages

FICTION

SAMAN
Ayu Utami
979-378011-8
2005, softcover, 184 pages

THE SPICE GARDEN
Michael Vatikiotis
979-97964-2-3
2004, softcover, 256 pages

THE KING, THE WITCH AND
THE PRIEST
Pramoedya Ananta Toer
979-95898-3-5
2001, softcover, 128 pages

IT'S NOT AN ALL NIGHT
FAIR
Pramoedya Ananta Toer
979-95898-2-7
2001, softcover, 120 pages

TALES FROM DJAKARTA
Pramoedya Ananta Toer
979-95898-1-9
2000, softcover, 288 pages

ILLUSTRATED

BANGKOK INSIDE OUT
Daniel Ziv & Guy Sharett
979-97964-6-6
2005, softcover, 176 pages

A CUP OF JAVA
Gabriella Teggia & Mark Hanusz
979-95898-9-4
2003, softcover, 144 pages

JAKARTA INSIDE OUT
Daniel Ziv
979-95898-7-8
2002, softcover, 184 pages

KRETEK: The Culture and
Heritage of Indonesia's
Clove Cigarettes
Mark Hanusz
979-95898-0-0
2000, hardcover, 224 pages

ACADEMIC

SOCIAL SCIENCE
AND POWER IN INDONESIA
Vedi R. Hadiz & Daniel Dhakidae
979-3780-01-0
2005, hardcover, 304 pages

PEOPLE, POPULATION,
AND POLICY IN INDONESIA
Terence H. Hull
979-3780-02-9
2005, hardcover, 208 pages

TRAVEL

THE NATURAL GUIDE
TO BALI
Anne Gouyon
979-3780-00-2
2005, softcover, 448 pages

COMMISSIONED

CHANGES & CHANCES:
A Personal History
of All Saints Jakarta
Andrew Lake
979-97964-9-0
2004, softcover, 240 pages

CELEBRATING INDONESIA:
Fifty Years with the
Ford Foundation
1953-2003
Goenawan Mohamad
979-97964-1-5
2004, hardcover, 240 pages

SOLSTICE

GOOD DAUGHTER
Bjorn Turmann
979-99888-0-2
2005, softcover, 352 pages

PT EQUINOX PUBLISHING INDONESIA
Menara Gracia, 6th floor
Jl. H.R. Rasuna Said Kav C-17
Jakarta 12940 - Indonesia
T : +62 21 522 0875
F : +62 21 522 0877
E : info@equinoxpublishing.com
www.equinoxpublishing.com